New Hampshire

A Bicentennial History

Elizabeth Forbes Morison
Elting E. Morison

W. W. Norton & Company, Inc.
New York

American Association for State and Local History

Authors and publishers make grateful acknowledgment to Sinclair Weeks, Jr., and to Dartmouth College Library for permission to quote from the Weeks Family Papers; and to Dartmouth College Library for permission to quote from the Diary of David Joseph Clark.

Library of Congress Cataloguing-in-Publication Data

Morison, Elizabeth Forbes.
  New Hampshire: a Bicentennial history.

  (The States and the Nation series)
  Bibliography: p.
  Includes index.
  1. New Hampshire—History. I. Morison,
Elting Elmore, joint author. II. Title.
III. Series.
F34.M67   974.2   76–4959

ISBN: 978-0-393-33410-4

Contents

Part I. Colony

Part II. State

Illustrations

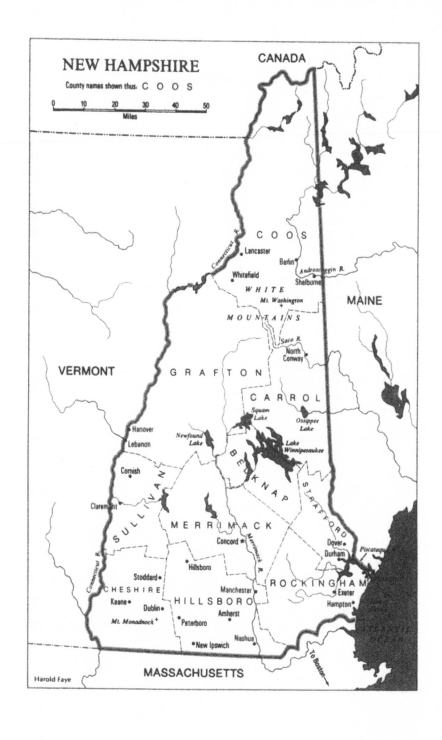

Invitation to the Reader

IN 1807, former President John Adams argued that a complete history of the American Revolution could not be written until the history of change in each state was known, because the principles of the Revolution were as various as the states that went through it. Two hundred years after the Declaration of Independence, the American nation has spread over a continent and beyond. The states have grown in number from thirteen to fifty. And democratic principles have been interpreted differently in every one of them.

We therefore invite you to consider that the history of your state may have more to do with the bicentennial review of the American Revolution than does the story of Bunker Hill or Valley Forge. The Revolution has continued as Americans extended liberty and democracy over a vast territory. John Adams was right: the states are part of that story, and the story is incomplete without an account of their diversity.

The Declaration of Independence stressed life, liberty, and the pursuit of happiness; accordingly, it shattered the notion of holding new territories in the subordinate status of colonies. The Northwest Ordinance of 1787 set forth a procedure for new states to enter the Union on an equal footing with the old. The Federal Constitution shortly confirmed this novel means of building a nation out of equal states. The step-by-step process through which territories have achieved self-government and national representation is among the most important of the Founding Fathers' legacies.

The method of state-making reconciled the ancient conflict between liberty and empire, resulting in what Thomas Jefferson called an empire for liberty. The system has worked and remains unaltered, despite enormous changes that have taken place in the nation. The country's extent and variety now surpass anything the patriots of '76 could likely have imagined. The United States has changed from an agrarian republic into a highly industrial and urban democracy, from a fledgling nation into a major world power. As Oliver Wendell Holmes remarked in 1920, the creators of the nation could not have seen completely how it and its constitution and its states would develop. Any meaningful review in the bicentennial era must consider what the country has become, as well as what it was.

The new nation of equal states took as its motto *E Pluribus Unum*—"out of many, one." But just as many peoples have become Americans without complete loss of ethnic and cultural identities, so have the states retained differences of character. Some have been superficial, expressed in stereotyped images— big, boastful Texas, "sophisticated" New York, "hillbilly" Arkansas. Other differences have been more real, sometimes instructively, sometimes amusingly; democracy has embraced Huey Long's Louisiana, bilingual New Mexico, unicameral Nebraska, and a Texas that once taxed fortunetellers and spawned politicians called "Woodpecker Republicans" and "Skunk Democrats." Some differences have been profound, as when South Carolina secessionists led other states out of the Union in opposition to abolitionists in Massachusetts and Ohio. The result was a bitter Civil War.

The Revolution's first shots may have sounded in Lexington and Concord; but fights over what democracy should mean and who should have independence have erupted from Pennsylvania's Gettysburg to the "Bleeding Kansas" of John Brown, from the Alamo in Texas to the Indian battles at Montana's Little Bighorn. Utah Mormons have known the strain of isolation; Hawaiians at Pearl Harbor, the terror of attack; Georgians during Sherman's march, the sadness of defeat and devastation. Each state's experience differs instructively; each adds understanding to the whole.

The purpose of this series of books is to make that kind of understanding accessible, in a way that will last in value far beyond the bicentennial fireworks. The series offers a volume on every state, plus the District of Columbia—fifty-one, in all.

Each book contains, besides the text, a view of the state through eyes other than the author's—a "photographer's essay," in which a skilled photographer presents his own personal perceptions of the state's contemporary flavor.

We have asked authors not for comprehensive chronicles, nor for research monographs or new data for scholars. Bibliographies and footnotes are minimal. We have asked each author for a summing up—interpretive, sensitive, thoughtful, individual, even personal—of what seems significant about his or her state's history. What distinguishes it? What has mattered about it, to its own people and to the rest of the nation? What has it come to now?

To interpret the states in all their variety, we have sought a variety of backgrounds in authors themselves and have encouraged variety in the approaches they take. They have in common only these things: historical knowledge, writing skill, and strong personal feelings about a particular state. Each has wide latitude for the use of the short space. And if each succeeds, it will be by offering you, in your capacity as a *citizen* of a state *and* of a nation, stimulating insights to test against your own.

James Morton Smith
General Editor

Part I

Colony

1

The Land

*O*NE must begin with the land, if only because so many men and women in New Hampshire for so long made their living off it. The soil, as the first settlers who came from England often described it, is thin, "cold," and strewn with rocks. On such ground succeeding generations built, in the sweat of their faces, the structure of landscape that is still well known: the lowland meadows; the upland pastures threaded with stone walls; the wood lots of pine, spruce, maple, birch, and ash; the sheds and barns of weathered board; the small white clapboard houses beneath the elms or spruces in the dooryard. These farms, by the principle of early settlement, were built on divisions of land called townships. The roads that pass by their often lonely sites lead, therefore, to places of more concentrated settlement, to the towns that support the farms with goods and services and set the organization for the farmers' political and social life. Here were built, in neat rows, the white houses; the shops of wood, brick, or granite facing; the Town House as the seat of government and the Meeting House with its steeple pointing to the sky.

Taken altogether, it is a structure of landscape that, more than the plantation, the ranch, or the great farmlands of the western prairies, has profoundly affected the American imagination. It is all mixed up in a confusion of memory with the Pilgrims, and Yankee ingenuity, and laconic wit, and the concept of town meeting and freedom to worship God, and Bunker Hill, and stopping by a wood on a winter's evening. Part of its hold is that it gives some sort of focus to such insecurely held pieces of historical experience. But it also lays its own claims upon the imagination. It is a landscape almost perfect in scale and in proportion. Whether it appears in the paintings of Abbott Thayer, or the photographs of Wallace Nutting, or as described in a play by Thornton Wilder, or on the calendar of a pharmaceutical firm, or even under direct observation by a summer tourist, the landscape is a frame for the local and the personal. It is a resolving organization, again in due proportion, of the devices of men and the powers of nature.

By distance, by infinite repetition, and by virtue of the fact that the world in its daily operations has moved far beyond such limiting dimensions and ratios, this landscape is now losing much of the force it used to exert on the American imagination. But, something between a fact and an illusion, it still establishes a dominant pattern on the land of much of New Hampshire. Though most of the farmers are gone, farm structures in various states of decay or sophisticated renovation remain on many hillsides. Though there are cities and suburbs, more people still live in the towns at least part of the time.

Within this dominant pattern, however, there is and always has been room for dramatic variation. Almost everywhere throughout the state there are to be found those high wooded hills or small mountains that introduce a pleasing unevenness or put a boundary on the local scene. Some—Chocorua, Kearsarge, Monadnock—stand out higher and alone and serve as organizing principles for the rolling land around them. And then there is the great range—the White Mountains—that many efforts at comparison and at more direct description suggest can never be adequately described. They are a special state within the state.

Beyond them lies Coos County and the North Country. Here New Hampshire looks about as it did when the first settlers came. What they saw, for the most part, was trees. In those first days, it is reported that of the 6 million acres now within the state's borders not much more than 1,000 acres were open land. The essential task, before all others, was, therefore, to clear out room to move around. For two hundred years men worked to cut back the trees to make way for hay meadows, dwelling places, and mill sites. By 1850 about half the state had been cleared of timber. But even so trees were everywhere—a sentinel pine, a brace of wineglass elms, a row of maples, a family woodlot, a larger, untended stand of pine, spruce, and hardwood. Then slowly, as people began to move off the farms, the trees grew in again. Today more than 80 percent of the land is wooded.

Much of that wood is in the North Country. From the beginning, this place had the quality of a fastness, a whole region remote, wild, apart, invested with the darkened silences of the unbroken forest. It still feels primeval. Few people, when they think of New Hampshire, think of the North Country, but it takes up a good part of the top third of the state.

Mountains, trees, and also water. Everywhere within the borders are running brooks, and almost anywhere one comes, in time, upon small ponds reflecting on their flat surfaces the scrub pines that rim the shores and the outlines of hills that rise around them. Near the middle of the state, just this side of the southern slope of the White Mountains, is the lake country—Squam, Ossipee, Newfound, and the long, striking reach of Winnipesaukee. Taken together, they are an arresting modification in the pleasant stretch of hills, fields, and woods and, taken with the mountains that lie just beyond them, they create a whole region of specialized attraction.

Out of Lake Winnipesaukee flows a river that bears its name. It runs south to the city of Franklin where it joins the Pemigewasset to form the Merrimack. The Merrimack proceeds due south down through the center of the state. From the swift flow of this beautiful river was taken, more than a century ago, the energy that brought the full force of the industrial revolution to bear upon the rural landscape. Passing through Manchester and Nashua, the Merrimack thus introduced the state to the way the rest of the world was beginning to make things, while separating those who lived along its banks from the way the rest of the state was continuing to live. The mills, the shops, the factories, the cities spreading out from this river are still an enclave.

There is another river. Taking its rise in a lake at the very top of the state in the bleakest part of the North Country, the Connecticut soon assumes a gracious course that becomes the western boundary of the state. Along the rolling hillsides of its valley lies the best farmland in New Hampshire. As a matter of fact, they still farm here. This land is part of a region half of which lies across the stream in Vermont. Long ago, it was settled chiefly by men and women who came up the river from Connecticut. And the river for years was the source of its principal associations; it supplied the means of transport to out-of-state markets to the south and a connection to a different kind of world. The two small societies growing up along the opposite banks had much in common in point of origin, developing experience, and ways of life. So it is not surprising that those on the New Hampshire side seceded for a time ahd joined with their neighbors across the water. And the valley of the Connecticut seems still contained within itself, something like a distinctive province.

Beyond the brooks and ponds and rivers there is the sea. Tucked in at the southeastern corner of the state is a stretch of land that for eighteen miles touches the Atlantic Ocean. Much of that shoreline is sandy beach and salt marsh, but at its northern end, just beneath the Maine border, there is a deep-water harbor. For a long time, in the early days, the land around this harbor was the most important place—in terms of numbers, assembled skills, political action, trade, and money—in the state. The site of Portsmouth, the colonial capital, it was the center of things. And, as time went on, Portsmouth, as capitals and seacoast centers do, developed an atmosphere of worldliness and—in the matter of goods and services—of elegance. All these assets, natural and acquired, proved insufficient, however, when the energies at work in the interior began to expand. During the first half of the nineteenth century, the weight of influence shifted slowly away from the high-toned seacoast and into the grasp of tradesmen, millmen, and farmers to the west. The essential spirit of the state moved inland.

In its sum, this state—this small piece of land 168 miles long from top to bottom, ninety miles wide at its broadest point—contains, it must be obvious, remarkable variations in its total landscape. And, by action of the four seasons, these variations are made to extend still further the range of its variety. Monadnock in a mantle of snow in the crystal light of winter is quite another thing from Monadnock in the baking heat and humid air of the early dog days; Winnipesaukee shining in a summer sun is not Winnipesaukee lying blue in the autumn foliage that burns on the surrounding hills. It happens even in the least of places— an old field shrouded in the first mist of the evening, lying beneath the drifted snow, or flat grey against a dead grey sky is three different places. The weather is forever shifting scenes and accentuating differences. There are no constants except in November's steady dreariness and in the endless blear of March.

The object here has been to suggest that, within the received impression of the classic structure of the landscape as a place of barns, weathered wood, white clapboard, and slender steeples, there is room for important variations and departures from the norm—east, west, north, south, and right down the middle. As the topography varies, so do the several states of mind—Berlin, "capital" of the north, is not and never has been like Portsmouth, once "capital" of the south. The mills along the Merrimack are not and never have been like the great farms along the Connecticut. The life of the state has been an uneven oscillation among different interests and energies more often than it has been a coalition of forces. Accentuating this situation has been the abiding tradition of the local and the personal first established by the principle of the individual township, and fortified by the common experience of the long years when farming was a way of life.

Amid these conditions of diversification and localization there was, at the very beginning and for a long time thereafter, a unifying influence—which was also, in a way, the product of topography. Perhaps the most important feature of the landscape, certainly in the first days, was the little strip of eighteen miles along the sea. Through that small aperture, the first settlers entered the state—not as refugees or reformers or spillovers from some previously settled colony—but as men who had set out from the home country to find their own place to pursue their own particular worldly purposes. Arriving on their independent mission they worked hard to construct a community of their own. Amid the pressures exerted by surrounding nature, the expanding province to the south, and the acquisitive instincts of their native land across the sea they demonstrated, after many vicissitudes, that they had built a society that could, by taking the necessary thought and action, take care of itself.

2

Tangled Boundaries

A glance at the map of New Hampshire would lead the uninitiated to conclude that the state, at one time or another, must have been awarded a corridor to the sea by Maine and Massachusetts. Considering the hundreds of miles of coastline bordering the two neighboring states, the eighteen-mile New Hampshire corridor is small, but it boasts one of the finest natural harbors in New England—Portsmouth—and its lower end defines exactly the point above which the famous white pines grow. In actual fact, New Hampshire's claim to this stretch of coastline was established when its first colonists landed there. For more than a century, European explorers had been cruising the shores of New England. Fishermen had come to the Grand Banks off Newfoundland in the early sixteenth century, and by 1600 England was ready for serious colonization backed by wealthy individuals anxious to tap the virgin resources said to be waiting in the New World.

In 1614, Captain John Smith explored and mapped the area from Penobscot to Cape Cod and made a report to Prince Charles, son of King James 1, who dubbed it New England. Then, in 1620, King James set up "the council established at Plymouth, in the county of Devon, for the planting, ruling and governing of New England in America." [1] This council, a

---

1. Jeremy Belknap, *The History of New Hampshire*, 3 vols. (Boston: Belknap and Young, 1791–1792), 1:5.

closed joint-stock company made up of forty men of wealth and noble rank, was headed by Sir Ferdinando Gorges. The territory under its jurisdiction was defined as the land along the seaboard between forty degrees and forty-eight degrees north latitude, extending from the Atlantic to the Pacific. By its authority, the initial New Hampshire settlements received their legal charters. The original grants made by the council were to become the most controversial in the state's history and were ultimately responsible for the peculiarity of the tiny coastline.

No story of New Hampshire can possibly be told without beginning with the Mason Grants, as they are called. "The history of the Mason Grant[s] is founded upon confusion and obscurity," according to Otis Hammond, who wrote the definitive study of the subject. Hammond blames the Council of Plymouth—"itself a confessed failure after only fifteen years of aimless floundering existence" [2]—for the confusion, and for the fact that New Hampshire's history revolved for decades around the attempts of succeeding generations to bring order out of the chaos that had been created.

Captain John Mason, governor of Newfoundland from 1615 to 1621, was an able, energetic, and ambitious man of considerable means who saw the potential, economic and sociological, in establishing and maintaining permanent settlements in New England. At thirty-four years of age—in a businesslike, responsible, and imaginative way—he proposed to establish well-rounded colonies of about seventy settlers plus tradesmen whom he would supply with tools, animals, food, and raw materials from England. His first application to friends on the council for a grant of land for this purpose was approved in 1621.

After this first grant, Mason teamed up with Gorges, and the remaining grants were made to the two of them. The five parcels of land awarded to these men included the area between the Naumkeag (now Salem) and Sagadahock rivers, and were bounded on the east by the Atlantic Ocean. Their western boundaries were imprecisely defined, but in general were not to be farther inland than sixty miles. One of these tracts, situated

2. Otis Grant Hammond, *The Mason Title and Its Relations to New Hampshire and Massachusetts* (Worcester, Mass.: The American Antiquarian Society, 1916), p. 3.

between the Merrimack and Piscataqua rivers, was to be named New Hampshire in honor of Mason's home county of Hampshire. Because the Englishmen making these awards had never been to America and knew almost nothing about the topography of the area, their grants of land were crudely delineated. Boundary decisions—who would receive what and how much—seem to have depended more on personal friendships than on geography. The net result was that overlapping and conflicting simultaneous grants were made, creating chaos for future generations.

To finance, populate, and administer these territories, Mason and Gorges formed the Company of Laconia in 1622, made up of British merchants from London, Bristol, Exeter, Plymouth, Shrewsbury, and Dorchester—place names that soon made their way to the New World and remain familiar today throughout the New England states. It quickly became apparent that setting up and maintaining even a small colony was more costly than anticipated and that absentee owners at such long remove could not always be sure that business was being conducted by their agents in the most industrious manner. After a few years, as the English investors began to complain of lack of return on their money, the Laconia Company was dissolved, and Mason and Gorges agreed on a division of their holdings. Gorges took the most northern parcel known as the Province of Maine, thereby establishing the northern end of the New Hampshire coastline. Maine was to remain a part of Massachusetts until 1820, when it obtained separate statehood. Mason was left as almost the sole proprietor of the rest of the extensive but tangled holdings which, to that point, had drained his resources to the tune of £22,000.

His grandiose plans for founding a hereditary principality in America might even then have been realized had he not suddenly died in 1635, leaving a widow, a daughter, and two very young grandsons. None of them had either the interest or the ability to carry out his plans. His estate was left to the grandchildren with the understanding that the eldest grandson would take the name of Mason when he came of age in 1650. The validity of Mason's claims to his vast holdings, and their subsequent disposition, were to be the source of endless altercation and political confusion, tying up hundreds of acres of land for almost 125 years. The litigations, changes of ownership, sales, claims, counterclaims, comings and goings of Mason descendants trying to secure their inheritance—and the boundary and border disputes that resulted—are an inextricable part of New Hampshire history. Ironically, except for the fact that the state was named for his native province, Mason and his enlightened plan for colonization and hopes for wealth and a substantial family domain in America are evident today only in the existence of a very small southern New Hampshire town that bears his name.

However, the settlements started by the Laconia Company at the mouth of the Piscataqua survived—despite the initial problems of the original grantees—and New Hampshire took root. From these first sparse footholds along the seacoast, in which simple survival was the most important concern, the evolution to statehood as it exists today seems to have had an organic logic of its own—sometimes paralleling the experiences of the other colonies but more often pursuing its own idiosyncratic course. Very shortly, other small towns in the coastal area were laid out. In 1633, besides Portsmouth (known for many years to the fishermen as Strawbery Banke), there were Northam, Hampton, and Exeter, all named by the gentlemen of the Laconia Company. Exeter had been founded by John Wheelwright and a small group after he had been banished from Massachusetts Bay for religious reasons. They had purchased the land for this settlement directly from the Indians, not realizing that it was part of one of the original Mason Grants. According to the deed, Exeter and the neighboring towns were to be governed by the colony of Massachusetts until they could set up a form of government acceptable to them all. By 1640, almost all the population of the province—approximately 1,000 hardy folk—lived in the area.

In 1641, having been unable to agree among themselves on a mutually satisfactory system of government, the residents decided to seek protection under the wing of Massachusetts: "To be ruled and ordered, in all causes criminal and civil as inhabitants dwelling within the limits of Massachusetts Bay.'' [3] For almost forty years they remained in uneasy, sometimes rebellious, but necessary conjunction, until, in 1679, the crown ordained that these settlements should become a single province— thenceforth to be known as New Hampshire—with a president and council supported by taxes.

But in 1684, just before he died, Charles II suddenly revoked the old Massachusetts Bay charter with the idea of combining Maine, New Hampshire, Massachusetts, and later Rhode Island and Connecticut, into a political unit under a single jurisdiction. When James II became king in 1685, he adopted this plan to establish the Dominion of New England and added New Jersey and New York to the proposed union in 1688. Perhaps it was true, as has been suggested, that ''it had long been the intention of the King [Charles II] to unite all the Colonial governments in this country [America] under one Governor-General. The design was to introduce the alterations so gradually as not to excite any alarm.'' [4] At any rate, James II, inheriting his brother's ideas, took up the scheme with enthusiasm, and the period of tyranny and oppression that followed helped to sow the seeds for the American Revolution.

> The press was restrained; liberty of conscience infringed; exorbitant fees and taxes demanded without the voice or consent of the people. . . . It was pretended that all titles to land were annulled. . . . Landholders were obliged to take out patents for their estates that they had possessed for forty or fifty years. Town meetings were prohibited. [5]

The Reverend Jeremy Belknap's outrage suffuses every word of his vivid account of this regime. The colonists would not have stood it for long, but James II's downfall and flight from England in December of 1688 released them from this contrived union.

3. Ralph May, *Early Portsmouth History* (Boston: C. E. Goodspeed & Co., 1926), p. 135.

4. Nathaniel Adams, *Annals of Portsmouth* (Portsmouth: Published by the Author, 1825), pp. 86–87.

5. Belknap, *History of N.H.*, 1:233.

For the province of New Hampshire, the following period was one of peculiar difficulty. Harassed by the personal and selfish concerns of the Mason claimants, sporadically at war with the Indians, and only recently out from under the wing of Massachusetts, it had had no chance to establish a stable government. It therefore rejoined Massachusetts for a brief time, until William and Mary designated New Hampshire a separate royal province in 1691. At that point, there were only 209 qualified voters, and they were not in agreement on how to proceed. In addition, the finances of the province were in poor shape—a problem that would be chronic for a long time to come.

The vexations of the relationship between New Hampshire and Massachusetts exist to this day, but at no point were they more evident than in 1715, when a serious jurisdictional dispute erupted over the duties and relative powers of the governor of Massachusetts and his lieutenant governor—whose bailiwick was New Hampshire. The issue turned on whether the lieutenant governor should have the authority to administer as full-fledged governor in New Hampshire during the governor's absence. The matter came to a head when orders from the governor (then Col. Samuel Shute) were being ignored or actively disobeyed by the lieutenant governor (then George Vaughan). Within New Hampshire, the issue created dissension between Portsmouth and some of the newer towns, which were beginning to grow in strength and power and resented the assumption of supremacy by the inhabitants of Portsmouth, whose prejudices favored trading interests above those of agriculture.

Into this controversial and acrimonious melee stepped John Wentworth, appointed by the king in December 1717 to replace Vaughan as lieutenant governor. His arrival marked a turning point for New Hampshire. Wentworth, who was particularly interested in encouraging inland settlements, received an unexpected assist in 1719 when a new group of immigrants came to New Hampshire from Boston, where they had landed. Bringing a welcome new set of ideas and attitudes, as well as useful new expertise, the Scotch Presbyterians from North Ireland had come in search of a place where they could live their own lives in peace and independence. The original 100 families—industrious, pious, self-respecting, brave, tough, and mostly illiterate—fanned out into several areas of New England. Sixteen families settled in the New Hampshire area just across the line from Haverhill, Massachusetts, and in the next few years, they were joined by many relatives and friends. In 1722, the New Hampshire town they had established was officially named Londonderry after one of their home towns in Ireland. The immigrants had arrived with potatoes for planting and the necessary materials for the manufacture of linen, including flax seed and foot-operated spinning wheels. Fortunately, the land proved satisfactory for both crops, and the town flourished. Others followed to this new territory, including some of the original seacoast settlers, or their children, who had outgrown the original land grants.

The focus of the state, however, was still along the coast, and the settlements to the west remained dependent on the seaport towns for necessities and for political leadership. During this period, Portsmouth, the seat of the government, was the acknowledged center of the province, both politically and financially.

As the province began to grow and prosper in the 1720s and 1730s, the main problem was to settle—once and for all—the boundary with Massachusetts, still in contention among Mason descendants and others. If New Hampshire was ever to have a governor of its own and achieve independence, as most of the population devoutly wished, the first order of business would be to provide a good, settled living and a chance of future financial gain for a prospective governor. To this end, it was clear, the territory which the settlers considered to be theirs, but which was also claimed by Massachusetts, must be obtained, defined, and put to use. Because Massachusetts was determined not to give up any land, the unfortunate colonists living in the disputed area were often taxed twice and were unsure what laws and regulations they were bound to obey. Sending someone in person to set their appeals before the king in England was too expensive for New Hampshire. Therefore, against the "vast, opulent, overgrown Province of Massachusetts . . . the poor little loyal distressed Province of New Hampshire'' [6] seemed to have very little chance of success. However, to the rage of Massachusetts and the amazement of New Hampshire, the crown in 1740 decided to take twenty-eight townships between the Merrimack and Connecticut rivers from Massachusetts and give them to New Hampshire, along with a vast fertile tract of land on the west side of the Connecticut River. By this decision, the province gained a total of 3,500 square miles and, in 1741, was at last freed to stand on its own feet, independent of Massachusetts. Benning Wentworth, son of Lt. Gov. John Wentworth, was named the first governor and remained at the helm for twenty-six years.

In 1746, as a last act in the seemingly interminable drama of the Mason holdings, John Mason, a great-great-grandson, sold out his inheritance to a syndicate of twelve Portsmouth men who called themselves the ''Masonian Propriety.'' After quitclaiming their rights in the existing towns of New Hampshire to the inhabitants, the proprietors chartered thirty-seven new towns. Their administration of what amounted to more than two million acres was considered by some to be a model of wise and purposeful public service, although they were accused by others of self-serving.

There were still areas to be dealt with, however, before the state could assume its final geographic form. A very complicated political negotiation was necessary to establish the western boundary. In 1741, the province was considered to extend to the edge of the next jurisdiction, which—at the time—was New York. But several township grants (known as ''New Hampshire Grants'') had been made in the 1740s and 1750s on both sides of the Connecticut River. The colonists who settled there were for the most part not related to the founding seacoast families, but had come up the river from Massachusetts and Connecticut. They therefore had more in common with people along both sides of the river than with the coastal population. As a result, a controversy raged for ten years over whether the towns on the

6. Belknap, *History of N.H.*, 2:154.

west side of the river should be under the jurisdiction of New York or New Hampshire. The king was again asked for a decision and, in 1764, he decreed that the western boundary of New Hampshire would be the western bank of the Connecticut River. By 1771, eight years after the conclusion of the French and Indian wars had stimulated a new wave of settlement, the population of the province had increased to such a degree that it was thought necessary to divide it into counties. Five counties were designated at this time and named after some of the governor's friends in England—Rockingham, Strafford, Hillsborough, Cheshire, and Grafton. All five were in functioning order by 1773. Town meetings were regularly held in the profusion of small towns that were chartered in this period; rudimentary rules and regulations were drawn up, and simple town elections were conducted. In early New England, a town was thought of as a political and social unit. The township served as a geographical designation.

The Revolution, while dislocating and financially draining the province, also brought a measure of new vitality to New Hampshire. With the withdrawal of supporting imports from Britain, such as hardware, sailcloth, and rope, the shipbuilding industry was forced to depend on local initiative. The same phenomenon obtained in the lumber and building trades, and all the inhabitants—particularly along the seacoast—had to think in terms of self-sufficiency to a degree hitherto unknown to them. Small, new, local industries were developed, the search for sources of iron and other raw materials was intensified, and many more farmers tried flax, hemp, and other crops in an attempt to broaden the scope of agricultural activities throughout the state. The population, which had been estimated at 82,000 at the beginning of the American Revolution, had risen to 142,000 in 1790. By 1800 it had reached 184,000—a thirty percent increase in a single decade. After the war, all ungranted crown lands were vested in the revolutionary government, and the state began incorporating new townships. Twenty-five were established, mostly through the center of the state, to accommodate the vastly increasing population. At the same time, the old, well-established towns began the process of subdividing into small townships, and some of the more recently settled ones almost doubled their populations in the twenty years between 1790 and 1810. Nearly the whole state—except for the areas of wilderness—had been marked off into townships by 1800.

The northern part of the state, which in the seventeenth and eighteenth centuries had been both forbiddingly wild and dangerously exposed to Indian and Canadian depredation, had a population of about 3,000 people by 1803. The dawning realization of the potential importance of the area—which had been vaguely included in Grafton County—and the increased size of its population convinced the authorities that it should be given county status. The "County of Cooss" was therefore established in March 1805. The name was derived from the Indian words *Cohos*, for a confederacy of tribes in northern New England, and *coo-ash*, meaning pines. The new county, with about 1 million acres of mountainous land—at that time mostly uncharted wilderness and primeval forest—was also the source of the Connecticut River. Since the remoteness of the area had precluded extensive surveys, the boundaries separating New Hampshire from both Maine and lower Canada were very hard to define. When Maine became a state in 1820, a joint commission was appointed to conduct a new survey and to install permanent boundary markers. The job was finally completed in 1858.

The boundary with lower Canada, however, was not so easily and amicably settled, because far more complicated and delicate issues were at stake. After the Indians had left and communications had been opened up, the northern area had attracted a variety of settlers. Some were drawn there by the fertility and beauty of the land, particularly along the Connecticut River and several small streams. Others came seeking a refuge beyond easy reach of the law, and many of these—during the first two decades of the nineteenth century—used the Canadian border area as a base for a lucrative smuggling business.

Inevitably, a boundary dispute arose between New Hampshire and lower Canada. According to the peace treaty with Great Britain signed in 1783, the northwest boundary of the United States had been established as the most northwestern head of the

Connecticut River, but there were differing opinions about which branch of which stream was the true head of the river. Both countries claimed the fertile Indian Stream territory, inhabited in 1831 by 360 people. These hapless individuals faced a situation resembling that of the settlers a hundred years earlier, who did not know whether they were under the jurisdiction of Massachusetts or New Hampshire. The Canadians attempted to compel some of the Indian Stream men to do military service, while New Hampshire tried to exact customs duties from them as they brought produce into the state. Small wonder that these independent people finally decided to form the "United Inhabitants of Indian Stream Territory" in 1832—with a constitution, assembly, and council—and to run themselves until the U.S. and Canada could resolve their differences. For three turbulent years, until considerable military force was brought to bear against them by U.S. authorities, they maintained their separate domain. At that point, those who wished to remain agreed to submit to New Hampshire governance, and the rest emigrated to Canada. The boundary was not officially and permanently fixed until 1840.

With the subdivision of the rest of the original counties into four more counties, the present ten counties of New Hampshire were complete. Sullivan County, made from part of Cheshire, was named for the Revolutionary hero, General John Sullivan, and incorporated in 1827. The next year, Merrimack County, formed out of pieces cut from Rockingham and Hillsborough, was established. In 1840, Strafford was subdivided to form two new counties. One was named Belknap County for the Reverend Jeremy Belknap, the great New Hampshire historian, and the other was called Carroll County for the last living signer of the Declaration of Independence.

By the middle of the nineteenth century, the population of the state had reached 318,000 and its area had been permanently established at 9,341 square miles. The present population is estimated at upwards of 780,000. The relative sizes of the principal cities of the state today indicate the shifts and changes that have occurred since the first settlers arrived at the Piscataqua. Manchester, on the Merrimack, leads, with 87,700 inhabitants, followed by Nashua with 58,500, Concord with 30,300, and Portsmouth with 25,500. After these, in descending order, come Keene, Dover, and Claremont. Hidden in these statistics are the stories of what happened in the state as it adjusted to the industrial revolution, making use—as it had before, but in a different way—of its great natural assets, the tumbling streams and swiftly flowing rivers.

3

First Settlements

I N 1621, when John Mason got his first grant of land in New England, he, the king, and a great many others in England thought that the American continent was going to make their everlasting fortune, and they wanted to be sure to claim it for Britain, for themselves, and forever. If their expectations of certain treasure (gold, for instance) were dashed on the reality, there was much more here than they knew. Money could be made on land speculation, for example—something that men living on a small island had never thought about. A true assessment of the economic potential in the New World was almost impossible, because only a few explorers and their crews had actually been there—and their reports were filled with honest misconceptions and some less-admirable misrepresentations. The interior of one of Mason's grants was described as containing

> divers lakes, and extending back to a great lake and river. . . . This river was said to be fair and large, containing many fruitful islands; the air pure and salubrious; the country pleasant, having some high hills; full of goodly forests, fair vallies and fertile plains; abounding in corn, vines, chesnuts, walnuts, and many other sorts of fruit; the rivers well stored with fish, and environed with goodly meadows full of timber-trees.[1]

1. Belknap, *History of N.H.*, 1:18–19.

The first explorers, in search of the "great lake" and hopeful of trading with the Indians, visited the White Mountains—describing them in equally romantic detail. But the country to the north was reported as "daunting terrible" although it might be a source of precious stones.[2] Mason, having been governor of Newfoundland, was in a far better position than his friends to guess at the harshness of the life to which he was sending his first New Hampshire settlers. He also knew the treasure that the sea offered to the rugged for the taking, and he must have been aware as well of the fortune to be made in peltry if the native trappers could be properly organized.

The only settlers actually outfitted and sent to America by the Laconia Company were two small groups established along the Piscataqua River in 1623. One was headed by David Thomson, and the other by Edward and William Hilton, all fishmongers from London. They were to establish permanent plantations and fisheries. The Hiltons went eight miles upriver to a place they called Northam (now Dover), while Thomson—who quit the province after a short time—started a plantation and built the first house on a commanding site in what became Rye. These people—the first New Hampshire colonists—started fisheries, erected saltworks for the preservation of their catch, and began trading with the Indians for furs. In time, more plantations were developed and wives and children—or women to become wives—came out from England on ships that also brought supplies to help transform raw coastal fishing stations into habitable settlements. Almost immediately, a few cargoes of fish and furs were sent back to England. The triangular trade that resulted—fish and furs from New England, slaves from Africa, and rum and sugar from the West Indies—was the first profitable venture for the New Hampshire settlers. (Unfortunately, black flies and smallpox reached New England from the West Indies in the same period.)

By 1632, however, the gentlemen of the Laconia Company were writing peevish letters complaining about the small return on their investment: "The adventurers here have bine soe discouraged by reason of John Gibbses ill dealing with his fishing

2. Belknap, *History of N.H.*, 1:20.

voiage. We desire to have our fishermen increased.'' The crisp reply of their New England factor, Ambrose Gibbons, suggests some of the problems of absentee ownership and control: "A Londoner is not for fishing neither is there any amity betwixt the West cuntriemen and them." Meanwhile, the settlers were requesting by every ship (but a round-trip to England in those days could be a matter of a year or more) additional equipment to pursue their fishing business and its adjunct industry, shipbuilding. Items such as nails, spikes, locks, hinges, ironwork for boats, twine, canvas, needles, cordage, pitch and tar, grapples and anchors were desperately needed, and no possible substitutes were then available in the wilderness. In addition, the settlers asked for sugar, wine, raisins, and malt for beer; clothing—or cloth and findings to make it with; tools of all kinds; guns and ammunition; domestic animals and hay for feed; plants and seeds; and more skilled people—both men and women. "A good husband with his wife to tend the cattle and to make butter and cheese will be profitable, for maides they are soon gone in this country," pleaded Gibbons in answer to querulous letters from London.[3]

The establishment of the first settlements required a fortitude, physical strength, and determination difficult even to imagine today. "For myself, my wife and child and four men we have but a half a barrel of corn; beefe and porke I have not had but one piece this three months nor beare (beer) this four months. I nor the servants have neither money nor clothes," wrote one of the factors to the company in London. "More men I could have and more employ," he explained, and—in answer to the growing demand for remuneration: "You complain of your returnes; you take the coorse to have little; a plantation must be furnished with cattle and good hir'd hands and necessaries for them, and not thinke the great lookes of men and many words will be a meanes to raise a plantation," he chided.[4]

If the settlers grew anxious and panicky in the first few years,

3. Belknap, *History of N.H.*, 1: Appendix, vi, viii, xvi. This appendix consists of a series of letters exchanged between members of the Laconia Company in England and their agents in New Hampshire. All further citations in this chapter are to letters in this series.

4. Belknap, *History of N.H.*, 1: Appendix, ix, ix, viii.

so did the members of the Laconia Company, as their money poured out in a seemingly endless stream. Almost from the beginning they received shipments of beaver, otter, marten, raccoon, and black fox skins, but the amounts never satisfied the voracious home office. "We hope you will find out some good mines which will be welcome newes unto us," wrote the disappointed investors, who still believed that fortunes in gold were available in America for the mining. Dutifully, Gibbons replied that they were shipping some ironstone that had been discovered. When he sent some stones from the White Mountains, the reaction from England was discouraging: "The christall stoans you sent are of little or no valew unless they were so great to make drinking cuppes or some other workes, as pillers for faire lookeing glasses, or for garnishinge of rich cabinets. Good iron or lead ore I should like better if it could be found." [5]

While the pull and tug continued between the conflicting interests and needs of New Hampshire and the mother country, the original settlements were growing. To stock the plantations, Mason sent out some Danish cattle which adjusted well to the new climate and were useful in hauling lumber. A profitable export item, they were driven to market in Boston, sent from there fresh to Nova Scotia and in salted form to the West and East Indies. Oxen were imported for heavy-duty work, since horses, at that point, were considered neither useful nor necessary. Sheep for wool and food, chickens for eggs and meat—all arrived by boat. By today's standards, they would probably seem very scrawny, but they throve. The great problem in the beginning was to feed them all, since pastureland and hay crops were limited. A small area of salt marsh around Hampton proved to be a valuable source of hay, but most feed had to be sent from England.

The first settlers, fishermen or Londoners with no experience in agriculture, animal husbandry, or wresting a living from a wilderness, found it hard to adapt to the new surroundings. They remained dependent on England for food supplies longer than would have seemed necessary, and it took them a long time

5. Belknap, *History of N.H.*, 1: Appendix, vi, xiv.

to learn how to use local resources, which were new to them. They were familiar with most of the local salt-water fish, but not with lobsters and clams. In the rivers, migratory fish such as salmon, shad, sturgeon, alewives, and lamprey abounded, and smaller streams provided many species of fresh-water fish—notably trout. Waterfowl of every description winged overhead. Wild turkeys of historic fame and impressive weight shared the forest with grouse, quail, and partridge, and wild animals—such as deer, moose, and beaver—were available for food and clothing. But catching and killing this abundance required specialized techniques unknown to most settlers and a constant supply of ammunition and tackle from England.

Berries and fruits were to be had for the picking, in season—grapes, black currants, raspberries, strawberries. Since many of the first New Hampshire inhabitants came from southwestern England, they were used to cider and perry—a fermented drink made from pears—and immediately requested apple and pear trees. As time passed, almost no plantation was without its orchard. Plums, peaches, cherries, quinces were all sent from home, but none did as well as the apples and white and red currants, which luxuriated in their new situation. The short New Hampshire growing season and sudden changes of climate usually reduced the yield of imported crops such as grain, flax, and succulent vegetables, and the settlers reported that these plants degenerated in several years: "The [grape] vines that were planted will com to little, they prosper not in the ground they were set, them that groo natural are veri good of divers sorts," wrote Gibbons in reply to enquiries from England about how things were faring.[6] As they explored further, other useful supplies were discovered—bayberry for candles, clay for ceramic vessels and bricks, ocher for colorings, soapstone for cleaning clothes, isinglass for windows in houses and ships, sulphur, and slate.

It is no wonder that the settlers who survived the first years implored the Laconia Company in London to send more men. It was a staggering job to carve plantations out of the wilder-

6. Belknap, *History of N.H.*, 1: Appendix, ix.

ness—simply to clear the smallest pasture for cultivation was an arduous task. In the fall, the trees had to be cut and burned, or girdled, to die and be burned another year. Then, after a spring rain, planting was done simply by putting seed in holes and crevices, since plowing was impossible until the rocks and stones had been dug out by hand and piled along the edge. It usually took three years to clear a rough pasture. Intervale land was the most productive, but for the earliest settlers little was available. Swamplands were excellent for grasses and, once they were drained, the dead trees were easily removed.

In addition to finding the means of subsistence in an unknown land with a reasonably unfriendly climate—for themselves and the various specialized workers who followed them to America—the settlers had to explore for exportable items, set up a fur-trading business with the Indians, establish a system of defense along the coast, and organize their settlements politically. The Laconia Company had decided to establish four towns along the seacoast, leaving it to the versatile factors to survey and define the boundaries and stake the claims. The task of reconciling the various overlapping jurisdictions would not have been easy, even if up-to-date surveying instruments had been available. One factor wearily commented on the difficulty of establishing a definite line between the Laconia patent and "the pattent of Bluddy Poynt, the river running so intrycate." The naming of many geographical points was left to the inspiration of the moment and to the uncertain spelling of the early surveyors. For instance: "Portsmouth runes from the harbor's mouth by the sea side to the entrance of a little river between two hed lands which we have given the names of the Little Bore's-hed, and the Grete Bore's-hed." [7]

Even as the expenses and headaches grew monthly more intolerable and the settlers began to lose their nerve, Mason seems to have remained firm and enthusiastic. In July 1634 he sent to his factor, Gibbons, as "a token from myselfe, one hogshead of mault to make you some beare" as an earnest of his determination and support. It must then have been a shock to Gibbons to

7. Belknap, *History of N.H.*, 1: Appendix, x, x.

receive the following letter from a superintendent with whom he had discussed all the needs and difficulties of the plantation in the summer of 1634 so that he could take a first-hand report back to Mason in London. The letter was dated April 1636: "Loveing frend Gibbens, Wee put into Ireland goinge home and there was taken sike (sick) and lefte behind, and laye so long before I got well that it was the latter end of December laste before I got to London, and Mr. Mason was ded." He had gone immediately to Gorges and the other investors but "they gave me no incouradgment for New England—So I suppose the affairs of Laconia is ded also. I intend to goe for the East Indyes." If the original settlers had not been extraordinarily resilient, this surely would have administered the *coup de grace* to the struggling New Hampshire colony. But, left high and dry, the inhabitants simply divided up Mason's property and belongings—without worrying about the legal niceties—and went their own ways.[8]

8. Belknap, *History of N.H.*, 1: Appendix, xiii, xvi–xvii, xvii.

4

The Indians

$\mathcal{N}$O narrative of the early settling of any state in New England can be complete without some consideration of the part played by the Indians. In the case of New Hampshire, they were of paramount importance and contributed much to the state's character. The initial dealings between settlers and Indians over land grants, according to early documents, were conducted in an honorable and businesslike way. The equal rights of the natives to live on and use the land freely—though not exactly to own it—were recognized. The Indians were necessary to the early settlers in many ways. Coexistence was mutually beneficial and, therefore, peace and mutual respect were essential.

In New Hampshire, there were two principal Indian confederations—the Abnakis in the east, and the Penacooks in the center and south—plus various other smaller tribes. There were fewer than 4,000 natives, mostly hill dwellers who practiced some rudimentary agriculture but were nomadic in habit. It was possible at first to establish contact with the sagamores of the tribes and to make agreements that acknowledged the rights and needs of both sides. The first deed entered into with them concerned a parcel of land bounded by the Piscataqua and Merrimack rivers, the sea, and carefully described inland boundaries, plus the Isles of Shoals. For the right to settle on and use this area, certain goods consisting of "coats, shirts, and kettles" were given to the Indians, who were to reserve to themselves free liberty of

hunting, fishing, fowling, and planting on these designated
acres. Since there were only a few-score square miles of cleared
land at the time of the first settlement, the Indians' insistence on
planting land is understandable and was happily acquiesced to
by the first settlers, who had no inclination toward agriculture in
any case. Rights in the land thus obtained by the English included all rights to natural resources found thereon and in the
ponds, rivers, and lakes, for whatever "use, benefits, profits,
privileges, and appurtenances." A deed was signed by the
negotiating Indian chiefs with their special symbols and by the
English through signature. Since the settlers were few, and were
clustered along the seacoast, there seemed every reason to believe that the agreement could go on forever, as stated. The Indians presumably welcomed an alliance with the English for
protection against the warlike depredations of other tribes and
were glad to establish trading outlets for their furs.[1]

How well the Indians really understood the agreements and
their implications can only be surmised. The original chiefs sitting down with the white men in oral and visible communication
may have formulated a comprehensible set of proposals that
seemed fair to both sides; but when the deed was translated into
English, written and presented for their "signatures," it had already moved into another reality more favorable to the settlers.
As long as the original "signers" lived, however, it is likely
that the rules were observed on both sides; for almost twenty
years, there was peaceful coexistence. After all, a London fish-
monger coming to the American wilderness in the seventeenth
century to set up permanent housekeeping needed an Indian for
a friend.

The English learned a great deal about "processing" the wilderness from Indian lore. Knowledge of medicinal uses of
plants handed on to housewives and mothers eased pains and
possibly saved lives. Indian trails provided the first "roads"
back from the seacoast as the settlers probed inland for the
lumber and minerals that they had been exhorted to find and
exploit. Indian adaptation to the environment was ingenious,

1. Belknap, *History of N.H.*, 1:11; 1: Appendix, iii.

and Indian techniques of survival through the bitter winters were adopted whenever expeditions left the coast. The furs traded by the Indians turned out to be essential to protect the settlers against the unaccustomed weather and, in time, the white men learned Indian methods of trapping and killing the animals and birds so desperately needed for food and clothing. Supply ships from England or Virginia were infrequent and rarely came at all in winter, so the unfamiliar skills essential for survival had to be learned on the spot—and quickly.

Although the settlers owed much to the Indians, the temptation to take advantage of their illiteracy and inexperience was almost irresistible. The Indians realized that they were being exploited and were embittered by increasingly flagrant abrogations of the treaties. The settlers built dams in the smaller streams and rivers to power grist and lumber mills, thus disrupting the habits of the salmon, which, by 1750, left these rivers for good because of sawdust pollution. English seines obstructed Indian fishing in the Saco River; lumbering operations drove game deep into the wilderness; domestic animals brought by ship from England roamed at will and despoiled Indian corn fields. Impulsive actions on both sides caused a death now and then. While the government in England probably would never have countenanced widespread defrauding of the natives, had the abuses been known, the English investors were glad enough to have some return on ventures that had so far proved disappointing. Since there was no one sympathetic to the red men to report their mistreatment to English authorities, the Indians simply took things into their own hands in the only way they knew.

The first organized Indian rebellion—known as King Philip's War, for Philip, sachem of the Wompanoags—began in 1675. During the brief uprising of the tribes, the Indians "dispersed themselves into many small parties, that they might be the more extensively mischievous." [2] The first attacks, on a settlement on the Oyster River in what is now the town of Durham, were devastating—houses were burned, men, women, and children were killed, and captives were taken. Belknap, writing more

2. Belknap, *History of N.H.*, 1:134.

than a century later, described this momentous break in the peaceful lives of the New Hampshire colonists:

All the plantations at Pascataqua were now filled with fear and confusion. Business was suspended, and every man was obliged to provide for his own and his family's safety. Thus the labor of the field was exchanged for the duty of the garrison, and they who had long lived in peace and security were upon their guard night and day, subject to continual alarms and the most fearful apprehensions.[3]

The people of New Hampshire were not to be totally free of such alarms and apprehensions for almost ninety years.

The story of Major Waldron, commander of the militia, and his experiences with the Indians in New Hampshire illustrates almost every facet of Indian warfare. At the end of King Philip's War in 1676, Waldron had been instrumental in concluding a peace treaty with the Indians and had gained their confidence. Unfortunately, however, he then tricked some of them into captivity; seven or eight died, and others were sold into slavery. None of the Indians who had had anything to do with this outrageous incident forgot it, and thirteen years later, they took their revenge. By that time, the Indians had lulled Waldron into so total a sense of security that he ignored warnings of planned attacks on his garrison house and two others in Dover. On a June night in 1689, two squaws appeared at the gates of each garrison house and were given leave to come in and spend the night. They later opened the gates, and signalled the rest of the Indians waiting in the woods. When Waldron heard the Indians crowding into his garrison house, he jumped out of bed, grabbed his sword, and tried to drive them back. But as he was turning to get his gun, the Indians "stunned him with an hatchet, drew him into his hall, and seating him in an elbow chair on a long table, insultingly asked him, "Who shall judge Indians now?" After dining on garrison victuals,

they cut the major across the breast and belly with knives, each one with a stroke, saying "I cross out my account." They then cut off his nose and ears, forcing them into his mouth; and when spent with

3. Belknap, *History of N.H.*, 1:137.

the loss of blood he was falling down from the table, one of them held his own sword under him which put an end to his misery.[4]

They also killed his son-in-law, took captive his daughter and grandchild, and set fire to his house. The other garrison houses received the same treatment, and in the course of the raid, twenty-three people were killed, twenty-nine were taken captive, and several houses were plundered and burned. One final event of the engagement, however, illustrates another side of the Indian character. While the raid was going on, a mother and her children, returning from Portsmouth, came upon the ghastly scene. She was so overcome that she sent the children and their companions to hide, as she lay down in the bushes expecting the worst. But she, her family, and her house were saved, because one of the attacking Indians, whom she had aided to escape after Waldron's trickery in 1676, recognized her. He had vowed at the time that he would never kill her or any member of her family.

The settlers' problems with the Indians were intensified by the competition for dominance between the French and British around the world. This competition seemed at first to be remote from the struggling settlements on the New England coast, but because of the French colony in Canada—with its influence by way of the St. Lawrence, the Great Lakes, and the Mississippi to Louisiana—the Franco-British conflict inevitably affected the northernmost British colonists. Recognizing the resentment and restlessness of the Indians around the edges of the New Hampshire settlements and realizing that a short war had already been fought, the French decided that the red men could be trained and manipulated for use against the British on the North American continent. At little expense and even less danger to themselves, the French set out to gain the confidence of the Indians. Jesuit priests, whose missionary zeal was such that they were willing to live and work closely with the natives while converting them to Roman Catholicism, were unwitting agents who convinced them that the British were "heretics." The corollary, of course, was that to break faith with or to kill a heretic was

4. Belknap, *History of N.H.*, 1:248–249.

not a sin. The Indians were trained by the French military to vent their legitimate grievances actively against the English colonists and were thus turned into a ruthless striking force under French command. Armed, sustained, and protected by the French, the natives were a devastating factor in the long struggle that began in 1689 with the declaration of King William's War. New Hampshire bore the brunt of their attacks as they poured down out of Maine and Canada in fearsome surprise raids. The history of every town, village, and outpost is darkened by laconic accounts of settlers killed, scalped, or taken prisoner as they went about their daily rounds. The actual number killed or captured at any one time was not great, but these swift raids were a far more effective means of harassment than full-scale attacks. "The wonder is that the outlying settlements were not abandoned. These ghastly insidious and ever-present dangers demanded a more obstinate courage than the hottest battle in the open field," observed Francis Parkman, as he considered the life of New England settlers in that period.[5] The spread of colonization to the north—and even to the west—was sharply curtailed, as many settlers lost their nerve and returned to less vulnerable areas. It became clear that community safety required the building of stockade garrison houses in every village, to which all could withdraw at night with sentries on duty. For the most part, the garrison houses were built by all inhabitants, who shared the labor and duties equally. These houses, usually surrounded by palisades, had loopholes for shooting, and the upper stories extended over the lower ones so that defenders could shoot down on attackers beating at the doors or laying combustible materials around the foundations.

During the early eighteenth century, the French gradually modified their style of warfare, changing their earlier emphasis from harassment and killing to taking as many live prisoners as possible. The goal was to provide a labor force for the French in Canada, and as the wars went on, bounties paid for able-bodied

5. Francis Parkman, *A Half-Century of Conflict; Part 6: France and England in North America*, 2 vols. (Boston: Little, Brown and Co., 1901), 1:51.

British men, women, and older children were high. Captives were also a source of provisions and revenue for the French, who freed those fortunate enough to have relatives or friends of means to pay their ransoms. One such captive wrote to his father in 1712:

Sir—I am in the hands of a great many Indians with which there is six captains. They say that what they will have for me is 50 pounds, in good goods, as broadcloth, some provisions, some tobacco pipes, Pommisstone [pumice stone], stockings, and a little of all things. Pray, Sir, don't fail for they have given me one day.[6]

The father did not fail, and his son returned unharmed—only to be killed several weeks later.

"A return from the dead was not more welcome than a deliverance from Indian captivity." [7] For women and children, the ordeal of the journey to Canada in the uncertain care of the Indians was the severest test of all. The story of one woman prisoner is typical:

Half starved and bearing a heavy load, she followed her captors in their hasty retreat towards Canada. After a time she was safely delivered of an infant in the midst of the winter forest; but the child pined for sustenance and the Indians hastened its death by throwing hot coals into its mouth when it cried.[8]

The woman herself survived and was finally ransomed by her husband.

Famine was a common attendant on these doleful captivities. The Indians when they caught any game, devoured it all at one sitting, and then girding themselves round the waist, travelled without sustenance till chance threw more in their way. The captives, unused to such canine repasts and abstinences, could not support the surfeit of the one, nor the craving of the other.[9]

Belknap continues by detailing the "hardships of travelling half naked and barefoot through pathless deserts, over craggy moun-

6. Parkman, *Conflict*, 1:53.
7. Belknap, *History of N.H.*, 1:140.
8. Parkman, *Conflict*, 1:49.
9. Belknap, *History of N.H.*, 1:284.

tains and deep swamps . . . exposed by day and night to the inclemency of the [winter] weather, and in the summer to the venomous stings of those numberless insects.'' But it must be added that there were documented instances of humane treatment at the hands of specific Indians, and that one agony was spared the women and girls. According to a Frenchman, writing of Indians in Canada: "There is no example that any have ever taken the least liberty with the French women, even when they were their prisoners.'' Mary Rowlandson, captured at Lancaster in 1675, writes: "I have been in the midst of these roaring lions and savage bears, that feared neither God nor man nor the devil, by day and night, alone and in company; sleeping all sorts together, and yet not one of them ever offered me the least abuse of unchastity in word or action.'' [10]

In Lovewell's War (1720–1726), the settlers declared war on the Indians living in Maine under the guidance and influence of a Jesuit priest named Sebastian Rasle. Three expeditions led by Capt. John Lovewell, a colonist, were sent out to find and kill the red men in their own encampments. These and other concerted efforts were fairly successful and a great majority of the local Indians finally withdrew to a settlement near Montreal, where they were thenceforth known as the St. Francis Indians. The red men living in Canada continued to serve the French as mercenaries, and during quiet intervals in the conflict between the French and the English, they were trained in the most effective use of their guerilla skills.

By the time of King George's War (1744–1748), therefore, they were well prepared for their role against the New Hampshire colonists. During this phase of the over-all war, when the thrust shifted toward the frontier towns along the Connecticut River, many captives were taken. Massachusetts, which in 1736 had set aside four towns designated for the defense of the area, now strengthened and enlarged their fortifications as the Indian threat intensified. Charlestown, the name given somewhat later to one of these towns, was the scene of the most concerted French and Indian attacks. It was staunchly defended and held firm.

10. Belknap, *History of N.H.*, 1:285; 1:287n; 1:287n.

Although New Hampshire went through a series of stringent ordeals during this period, it also gained valuable experience—experience that would help to end the long, intermittent war and would also be of unique value during the Revolution. When, in 1752, John Stark was captured and taken to Canada by the Indians while on a fishing trip, he managed to pick up a great deal of information about the area between New Hampshire and the St. Lawrence River. Subsequently ransomed by friends and relatives, he brought this knowledge back with him, along with an understanding of Indian methods of warfare and possible ways to combat them.

By 1754, Indian attacks along the Connecticut River and the Merrimack Valley had become so widespread and occurred so frequently that the other New England colonies could no longer ignore them as frontier skirmishes. Although France and England were formally at peace, it was clear that France was girding for another onslaught. A convention of delegates from the seven provinces was therefore called—meeting in 1754 at the Albany Congress to plan joint countermeasures in the event of new war with France and her Indian allies. The special experience and hard-won skills of the New Hampshire men became apparent when Robert Rogers organized his Rangers—a New Hampshire group that served for five years as scouts and spies for the British in the Lake Champlain area. In 1759, the Rangers destroyed the home base of the St. Francis Indians. Other New Hampshire men attacked and captured Crown Point on Lake Champlain and later constructed the eighty-seven-mile Crown Point military road—the first highway over the Green Mountains.

Peace finally came when a treaty was signed in Paris in 1763 between France and England. Although the French had been expelled from North America, and New Hampshire's long struggle against them and their Indian allies was over, the settlers had been forced to neglect their lumber and fishing trades and hundreds of domestic animals had been lost. Britain did attempt to reimburse the colonies for their aid in winning the war, but it has been calculated that New Hampshire paid £1,000 for every

Indian killed. Not even a fraction of these costs was covered by the British.

The long struggle against the Indians left a certain legacy of ill-will, but what endures today is the prevalence and preponderance, throughout the state, of Indian place names. The lakes, streams, and mountains that provide the state's most appealing and remunerative recreational facilities ring with the musical names given them by the Indians. It is possible to look at the mountains even now, to see them as the Indians must have seen them, and to understand why they were revered as the dwelling places of the spirits. It should also be possible to feel regret that the extinction of a race was part of the price our ancestors—however heroically—paid to establish themselves in the state.

5

Use of Resources

*T*HE original settlements in New Hampshire were financed by Englishmen of wealth and position who hoped to make vast fortunes out of the resources said to be available in New England. Captain John Smith, prospecting the shores of New England in 1622 in the interests of possible investors, had been enthusiastic about the excellence of the fishing: "Honorable and worthy countrymen, let not the meanness of the word FISH distaste you, for it will afford you as good gold as the mines of Potosi and Guiana; with less hazards and charge and more certainty and facility." [1] He also commented on the convenience of two harbors (later named Portsmouth and York) and noted that the area around Portsmouth was known as "Passataquack." His reports, together with those of other explorers who had also found the mouth of the Piscataqua River, convinced the Laconia Company that the first settlers should go there to fish.

The intricacy of the shore line which, according to William G. Saltonstall, in his *Ports of Piscataqua* stretches New Hampshires's official eighteen-mile coast to "at least 100 miles of inland shore washed by salt water," and the extensive shoreline of the Isles of Shoals provided dozens of sites for small

---

1. John Smith, *Works of Captain John Smith, 1608-1631*, edited by Edward Arber (Birmingham, England: The English Scholar's Library, 1884), no. 16, p. 272.

fisheries.[2] Salt cod, one of the first exports of the Piscataqua region, continued to be a major resource, but even as late as the Revolution, there was a serious shortage of salt. The colonists were always on the lookout for salt springs, and small salt works dotted the shore line near the fisheries. Even so, salt had to be imported for many years.

Fishermen went out daily in fall and winter in light, swift, whaleboats—pointed at both ends—and during the spring and summer seasons, they stayed out until the boats were filled. For trips to the Banks, three times a year, schooners of twenty to fifty tons were used. These schooners, manned by fewer than ten men, could bring in five to six hundred quintals (100 kilograms) of fish—split and salted on board. The catch, rinsed in salt water when unloaded, was spread out to dry on flakes— racks of brush supported by three-to-four-foot stakes. The spring catch was considered to be the choicest and was generally salted and dried and kept for Saturday eating by well-to-do New Englanders. Later catches were exported to Europe and the West Indies.

In Belknap's view it was

> in the power of the Americans to make more advantage of the cod fishery than any of the European nations. We can fit out vessels at less expense, and by reason of the westerly winds, which prevail on our coasts, in February and March, they can go to the banks earlier in the season . . . and take the best fish. We can dry it in clearer air than the foggy shores of Newfoundland and Nova Scotia . . . Salt can be imported from abroad cheaper than it can be made at home; if it be not too much loaded with duties . . . The fishing banks are an inexhaustible source of wealth; and the fishing business is a most excellent nursery for seamen.[3]

By the time the Revolution disrupted the American fishing industry, it had provided the base for many New Hampshire fortunes.

Fishing was not the only source of wealth in the province, however. The first settlers were instructed to make contact with

2. William G. Saltonstall, *Ports of Piscataqua* (New York: Russell & Russell, 1968), p. 3.

3. Belknap, *History of N.H.*, 3:216.

the Indians, to insure a steady supply of valuable furs, which fetched high prices in England and on the Continent. Indian trappers traded black fox, otter, beaver, marten, and raccoon—all native to New Hampshire—for various imported articles highly prized by them. For a considerable period, pelts were used as a form of money in the province, and the fur trade flourished as long as relations with the Indians remained stable.

"Shipbuilding was begun in America under the pressure of necessity, and it was fostered by the conditions of life in the new country." [4] This statement by Arthur H. Clark in a book on clipper ships, could as well have been made specifically about New Hampshire. From the beginning, fishermen needed whaleboats and schooners, and the men who explored the wilderness did so in birchbark canoes copied from the Indians. The province was a land of rivers, streams, and lakes whose importance became apparent when settlers began to move inland. To navigate these waters, the newcomers developed practical craft called "gondolas," which were little more than heavy barges. In their subsequent evolution, these boats became known as "gundelows," designed for shallow water, low and narrow so they could pass beneath bridges, which became more numerous as plantations proliferated inland. Heavily laden, bearing the commerce of the province, these craft provided outlets and connecting links with the seacoast. Ships of 200 to 300 tons needed for the triangular trade with the British "sugar islands" and England were also built from earliest times.

The New Hampshire lumber industry, founded by colonists struggling to survive, gradually developed into a world-renowned enterprise and a major source of the colony's income. Among the earliest settlers were skilled fishermen and lumbermen who understood the practical requirements for seaworthy ships and knew how to obtain the materials for them. In addition, there were prodigal quantities of durable, straight-grained white pines close at hand, as well as water power for processing cut timber. The streams and rivers that converged to form the Piscataqua district flowed swiftly as they dropped down to sea

4. Arthur H. Clark, *The Clipper Ship Era* (New York: G. P. Putnam's Sons, 1919), p. 2.

level and were easily harnessed to power sawmills. The first of these mills was built in the 1630s and, by 1700, ninety saw mills were operating in the region. With lumber and power readily accessible, the inhabitants of Portsmouth, Kittery, Dover, and Exeter all started small shipyards. Outside supervision of these numerous establishments to insure proper seaworthy construction was required under the provisions of a law passed in 1641 by the Massachusetts General Court. Sometimes small sloops were built deep in the woods, near the lumber supply, and hauled by teams of oxen down over the snow and out onto the frozen river ice, to be floated at spring thaw.

When shipbuilding developed into an industry that provided a commercial livelihood for the towns along the seaboard, Britain began to fear the expanding freedom and prosperity that it brought to her colony. As early as 1668, Sir Josiah Child, a director of the East India Company, complained that

> of all the American plantations, His Majesty has none so apt for building of shipping as New England, nor any comparably so qualified for the breeding of seamen not only by reason of the natural industry of the people, but principally by reason of their cod, and mackerel fisheries, and in my poor opinion, there is nothing more prejudicial and in prospect, more dangerous to any mother kingdom than the increase in shipping in her colonies, plantations, and provinces.[5]

It was obvious that England could not be guaranteed the full value of the goods produced in her colonies if they built their own ships and peddled their exports elsewhere. For the crown, another disquieting factor in the 1720s was a large-scale exodus from England of shipwrights and carpenters, who had seen their jobs disappear as more and more merchants ordered ships from American shipyards, where the availability of lumber measurably reduced the cost. Failing to get restrictions that would limit the size of American ships and force them to trade only with Great Britain, many London and Thames River shipwrights decided to take their chances in New England. All these developments challenged the British mercantilist view that the colonies

5. Clark, *Clipper Ship*, pp. 2–3.

should be a source of revenue to the mother country and that the seapower of England should at all times be protected and advanced.

The British navy never ordered ships from American shipyards, but the British merchant marine had no such prejudice; they ordered vessels freely. Local shipyards were also kept busy by a growing demand for passenger ships. By the 1760s, coastal passenger boats built in New Hampshire regularly plied between Portsmouth and Boston, and it was possible to book comfortable accommodations on a more irregular schedule south to New York and Philadelphia, north to Newfoundland and Nova Scotia, and across to Europe. The *Piscataqua Packet*, a particularly trim passenger vessel, was built and put into service at this time. For the New Hampshire coastal towns, the twenty-five years preceding the Revolution were a period of vigorous growth and expanding prosperity, with a strong emphasis on shipbuilding and trade. "The Piscataqua district in 1769 produced one third as many vessels [45] as all Massachusetts [137]." [6]

One serious weakness in the American shipbuilding industry had been its dependence on England for fittings and rigging. Sporadic efforts had been made to establish manufactories for ships' hardware, anchors, and shipwrights' tools, but the necessary raw materials were not readily available in quantity, and the local bog-iron was of poor quality. Similarly, attempts had been made to raise hemp and flax, and to build ropewalks and duck and canvas works. But, almost from the beginning, the provincial authorities had tended to neglect agriculture in favor of fishing, shipbuilding, and lumbering, and not enough land had been cleared to support huge and specialized crops. When the Revolution suddenly deprived the shipyards of necessary imports, the settlers responded with enterprise and imagination to keep the shipyards functioning in at least a limited way. By 1788, when a great victory parade was held in Portsmouth to celebrate the adoption of the Federal Constitution, representatives of every trade and calling were able to march with the

6. Saltonstall, *Ports of Piscataqua*, p. 54.

tools or symbols of their livelihood. The list included "Blacksmiths and Nailers with their forges, anvils and sledges; Shipwrights with their tools; Rope-makers with a spinning wheel and hemp around their waists; Instrument-makers with an Azimuth Compass; Carvers, Painters, Glaziers, and Plumbers." [7] Clearly, New Hampshire had made great strides toward practical independence.

"A Piscataqua vessel in the 1780's could be built for less than twenty-five dollars per ton. In view of the fact that English, French, and Dutch merchants had to pay fifty dollars per ton, it is natural that shipbuilding revived after the war." During the 1790s, shipbuilding and shipping both reached a new peak of prosperity: "Within ten years (1791-1801) the value of New Hampshire exports rose from $142,859 to $555,055." Still to come was the clipper-ship era, which brought additional prosperity to the shipbuilders of Portsmouth. Between 1800 and 1850, 486 vessels were built there—many of them on order for owners in Salem and Boston. After a final burst of activity in the 1850s, however, the demand for the old heavy clippers declined, and the yards fell gradually into disuse. Men who had built magnificent sailing ships of good New Hampshire wood found themselves masters of an anachronistic trade. They either converted their skills to other uses, or settled down to live out their days at ease—in beautiful houses, built with care and grace—beside a river whose name they had helped to make famous throughout the seven seas. [8]

One unique craft—the "mast ship"—was of signal importance to New Hampshire. Designed and built in quantity for 125 years in the Piscataqua region to carry pine masts to England for the British navy, theirs is a separate story. Of 400 to 600 tons or more, these ships had to be of the sturdiest construction, for the rigidity of their special cargo put an unprecedented strain on a ship, particularly in a storm. They were loaded through oversize ports in the stern and were handled at sea by about twenty-five men. Because of the enormous monetary value of their cargoes,

7. Adams, *Annals of Portsmouth*, p. 29.
8. Saltonstall, *Ports of Piscataqua*, pp. 121, 122.

they were sometimes escorted across the ocean by armed convoys. By 1670, Portsmouth was sending out ten mast ships a year.

The mast trade with England, for which they were built, was the most dramatic and politically important enterprise to occupy the New Hampshire colonists from 1640 to the Revolution. According to Robert G. Albion, in his book *Forests and Sea Power*, it represented only a tenth of total timber exports, but its drama came from the heroic scale of the mast pines themselves. The earliest explorers in the Piscataqua region had been impressed by forests that covered the land to the water's edge, and in particular by the extraordinary height and straightness of certain trees—which suggested masts to any seafaring man. Tales of these giants must have piqued the curiosity of the British navy officials in charge of building warships at the beginning of the seventeenth century. Since no such trees grew in the British isles, the navy had hunted them throughout the world and, as supplies dwindled, had been forced to construct composite masts by forming several layers of different woods around a central spindle, usually of fir. Their strength could not be compared with the strength of a so-called single-stick mast of good quality.

The mast pines of New Hampshire (*Pinus strobus*), stood singly, straight as soldiers, 500 to 1,000 years old, with no branches up to the crown. They were 36 to 75 inches in diameter at the base and 150 to 200 feet high—twice as tall as the trees around them. Getting such giants out of the forest was a complex and dangerous business. First, a tree was selected by sight, then tested by ear for solidity by thwacking it with an axehead. If a tree had decayed at the center and was therefore of no use as a mast, it made a hollow sound. Once a sound mast tree passed muster, its angle of fall and route to the sea were carefully plotted and prepared. Bushes and trees were felled to provide a bed on the side to which it would fall. Deep snow was an asset to cushion it and to blunt the rocks that might gash it. Snow also simplified the problem of hauling it out of the woods.

When all was in readiness, two axe men stepped up to fell the tree, butt end toward the sea. Swinging in perfect unison, making every stroke count, and shooting off chips as big as frisbees, the men gauged every inch and every angle with woodsmen's intuition and the precision of long practice. When they finally reached the heart of the tree, gravity did the rest. Once felled, cleared of branches, and inspected for unsuspected flaws, the great tree was finally loaded for its journey on a mast sled built for the purpose. "The process of hauling the pines to water and rafting them down to Portsmouth demanded above all a tremendous amount of brute strength. The diligent and patient New England ox was made for such work. Skillfully trained and handled, this massive animal was a mainstay of the mast trade." [9] Sometimes ninety to a hundred oxen, hitched up in a double string, were needed to haul in a single mast sled, so heavy was the giant log. On long hauls, as many as six or eight oxen would die from exertion, and replacements had to be kept always ready. Food for these animals was a constant problem and, when it was not available, lumbering operations had to be suspended.

The journey from the stump completed (and by 1700, good mast pines were as much as twenty miles or more into the forest), the stick arrived at one of the masthouses situated at the mouths of the rivers. There the pine was stripped of its bark, hewed into sixteen sides, and cut to the most advantageous length by mastwrights. The accepted rule was that an inch of diameter at the base should equal a yard of length. In other words, a thirty-six-yard mast would be made from a tree with a thirty-six-inch base diameter. The value of masts for export increased rapidly with their height. By the late seventeenth century, a tree that would bring £100 or more as a single-stick mast of the largest size would only be worth £15 as assorted lumber. The incentive to use trees to their fullest capacity, therefore, was great, but the lumbermen and others who prepared the trees for shipping did not share in the premium profits.

The masts were next loaded into mast ships waiting in the harbor. After 1652, when the mast trade was fairly well regulated, these ships were designed to hold forty to a hundred of the

9. Saltonstall, *Ports of Piscataqua*, p. 57.

longest masts, plus various shorter pieces for use in making yards, spars, and bowsprits. If no mast ships were available, the masts waited in large ponds that could store a hundred or more. (Similar storage ponds were waiting at the English shipyards.) Belknap's observations give a clue to the scale of the whole operation:

> Between the upper end of Great Island and the town of Portsmouth, on the southern side of the river, is a broad, deep, still water called "the Pool"; where the largest ships may lie very conveniently and securely. This was the usual station for the mast-ships of which seven have been loaded at one time.[10]

It was proven in practice that the average New England pine masts retained their strength and resilience four times as long as Norwegian ones that the British navy had been using. Presumably, an American mast would last in good condition for fifteen to twenty years. His Majesty's enemies, however, had learned that, while it was almost impossible to sink British warships in sea battles because of the strength of their oaken hulls, shooting out their masts and spars seriously disabled war vessels. Consequently, after battle, the ships would limp home for repairs, and a great reserve of masts and spars of all sizes was needed. By 1691, "the trade in New England mast pines was considered vital to the Royal Navy's survival, which accounts for the strong measures taken in the 18th century to safeguard it."[11] The British demand for masts became ever more importunate: historian Joseph J. Malone estimates that, between 1694 and 1775, about 4,500 masts were shipped to England. When, by 1750, the New Hampshire supply was virtually exhausted, the search eastward for lumber of mast dimensions launched the colonization of Maine.

It is hard to pinpoint the moment when masts ceased to be one of New Hampshire's best exports, and the mast trade became a bone of contention and a liability for the province. From 1691 on, England had attempted to insure her supply by prohi-

10. Belknap, *History of N.H.*, 3:198.
11. Joseph J. Malone, *Pine Trees and Politics* (Seattle: University of Washington Press, 1964), p. 47.

biting the cutting of pines over a certain size by any unauthorized person, and by fining colonists who disobeyed the rule. In 1729, as England's insatiable need for masts and pine lumber for all forms of shipbuilding grew, the British devised a scheme: the best pines in the American forests were marked with a "Broad Arrow" made with three chops of a marking hatchet. The sign, cut into the trees by English surveyors, looked like the barbed head of an arrow or a crow's track. No tree bearing this mark was to be cut by the settlers for their own use on pain of a rigorously enforced £100 fine. But depredations continued, and the king set up the office of Surveyor General of His Majesty's Woods and Forests in America to enforce compliance with the rules, to seize illegally cut lumber, collect fines, and prosecute offenders.

As the eighteenth century progressed, however, the needs of the colonists for pine lumber for their own shipbuilding, dwellings, and public buildings became equally urgent. In addition, the colonists were hard put to maintain the huge lumbering crews needed to fill British orders because the more pressed the British navy was in times of crisis, the more lax it was in paying its bills. Armed protection also had to be provided by the colonists for the lumbermen during periods of alarm over Indian attack, or they would refuse to go very far afield. For these and other reasons, the colonists resented the Broad Arrow policy and used every stratagem to evade and subvert the system.

Luckily for the inhabitants of the province, Britain had little interest in any lumber other than pine, and a wide variety of useable trees grew in the woods. A simple sawmill with a single vertical saw could be set up wherever there was a stream with enough current to power it; the wood could easily be milled where it fell; and the rig could be quickly moved farther upstream when the supply was exhausted. Virtually everything needed by the early colonists had to be made from wood. By trial and error, and some observation of Indian methods, basic articles were developed in the wood best suited to their purpose. Native oak went into the hulls of colonial ships. Staves of oak were formed into casks, barrels, and hogsheads in which everything from molasses and rum to corpses, lime, meat, bread, and even water was stored. Firkins, pipes, and clapboards were also cut from oak. Oars were made of ash—as were fence rails, handles for tools, and frames for plows, carts, and sleighs. Elms, not usually thought of as "working trees," produced chair bottoms and bed cords, and—because their wood is not easily split—the hubs of wheels. Hemlock, which held nails well, was widely used for building and was tough enough for flooring bridges, wharves, and barns. Chestnut was found to be the best for fencing; and windlasses, wheels, and blocks were fashioned out of rugged buttonwood lumber. Agricultural implements, large and small, were made from a variety of woods.

In the second half of the eighteenth century, small enterprises providing employment and a modest livelihood for families, or an entire township, could be based on a particular product made from a locally abundant wood. Birch, both white and black, lent itself to this sort of industry—such homely items as shoe pegs, spools, clothespins, and toothpicks could easily be fashioned of this material. Following the example of the Indians, the colonists made dishes, boxes, and canoes from white birch bark. Boxes of birch or pine in all sizes and shapes were popular and saleable items. Baskets made of rushes or splints, obtained by pounding black ash sticks into flat ribbons with a maul, were widely made and very popular. Cabinetmaking, originally a necessity, became both an art and a business. At least a dozen kinds of wood were used in turning out simple but handsome furniture—some of it still useable and highly prized today by antiquarians. Birch, maple, cherry, and pine were the most frequently used for furniture. In almost every community, people of all ages would work through the long winter months when outdoor projects were at a standstill. And when the supply of hand-crafted goods exceeded the local demand, such goods could be peddled elsewhere, or exchanged for similarly produced items from other settlements.

New Hampshire trees also provided a variety of important derivatives that were widely used by the colonists, and that often proved to be lucrative export items. Good charcoal, obtained from oak or pitch pine, was burned to smelt the local bog-iron used to make rude tools—two hundred bushels of wood at four cents a bushel produced enough charcoal to smelt one ton. Some of the peat taken from the swamps around Dover was also used as fuel. Maples could be converted into potash—the ashes, processed in huge kettles, had medicinal properties and could also be used to extinguish fires. Five to six hundred bushels of ashes were required to yield a ton of potash, but the product was in great demand, as was the more highly refined and valuable pearlash. Both were exported from earliest times.

British investors were both surprised and disappointed that the New Hampshire settlers were unable to satisfy the demand of England's shipyards for tar and pitch. There was, after all, no shortage of pitch pine knots and roots—a great source of terebinthine oil that could be converted into pine tar. And turpentine could have been extracted from every species of pine. Although English naval stores, as they were collectively called, seemingly could have been supplied, the colonists never mastered the distillation technique—which affected quality. Though given written directions by the British, they never produced enough tar and pitch to satisfy much more than their own needs. They were more successful, however, in collecting maple syrup and boiling it down into sugar.

> The sugar thus procured is an agreeable sweet, frequently supplying the place of milk and meat, and affording wholesome and nourishing food for children. The drainings of the sugar, or the last run of the sap, which will not granulate, are used as molasses to sweeten cakes, puddings, and other viands.[12]

The colonists enjoyed their maple products, but there is no record that they were ever exported in any quantity.

Although New Hampshire never proved to be a money-maker for England, many of its own inhabitants managed to amass substantial personal fortunes. Most of them lived along the seacoast in or near Portsmouth, which, by virtue of its great harbor, was the capital and financial nerve center of the province. Fishing, lumbering, shipbuilding, shipping, and commerce—all were focused on its bustling shore. Among the men who made

12. Belknap, *History of N.H.*, 3:115–116.

their fortunes in these varied enterprises were the individuals who later assumed political leadership. It seems, as one considers the evolution of the psyche of New Hampshire, that the natural characteristics of the province profoundly influenced the character of the men who were drawn to it. They did not impose their will on the land so much as the land imposed its character on them. After the Revolution, when the emphasis shifted from the coast, the sociology of the state changed completely.

6

The Wentworth Years

*T*HE province of New Hampshire survived its disorderly development in the seventeenth century because of the tenacity and stubborn strength of its colonists. The rough physical demands of the work done by most of them—fishing and lumbering—the harshness of the climate, and the daily threat of Indian raids in the second half of the century had left them little time for philosophic concerns. The province's equivocal status as a part of Massachusetts had not been conducive to the rise of strong local politicians. Moreover, its classification as a separate royal province in 1691 had been an attempt by the crown to curb the power of Massachusetts; it provided no real autonomy for New Hampshire. The colony did not offer a dazzling prospect to an English gentleman in search of a lucrative and powerful colonial governorship. As a consequence, those who had sought appointment as lieutenant governor of Massachusetts in charge of New Hampshire—particularly Mason descendants or their representatives—had had ulterior personal motives and had contributed only minimally to its well-being. But in 1717, a man appeared whose interests were truly those of New Hampshire, whose talents were supported by an equable temperament, and whose coming heralded a dramatic shift in the fortunes of the struggling province.

When John Wentworth, in that year, was appointed lieutenant governor by the king, the province had a population of about

10,000. Wentworth was the grandson of Elder William Wentworth, who had settled at Exeter in 1639; as a young man, he had taken to the sea and had made a substantial fortune as a merchant. "By a steady attention to business, and a prudent obliging deportment, he had recommended himself to the esteem of the people." [1] Having served for years on the New Hampshire council before his appointment, Wentworth understood the difficulties he would face, both in America and in England. The King's Broad-Arrow policy on the mast pines—proclaimed nine years earlier—had engendered widespread resentment; Indian raids were a continuing problem, and the argument with Massachusetts over geographic boundaries was a source of constant friction between the two provinces. Wentworth's even-handed dealings in negotiating with the Indians resulted in a peace treaty in 1725. But his primary interest—and the area in which he made his greatest contribution—was in putting the state on its feet financially. To this end, he fostered commerce and encouraged settlements as far as fifty miles inland. He died in office in 1730, but not before he and his wife had produced sixteen children, fourteen of whom survived. "The administration of Lieutenant Governor Wentworth gave a dignified beginning to the administrative record of his family which covered so large a part of the 18th century in Portsmouth." [2]

During the 1730s, the prosperity and prestige of Portsmouth continued to grow. New groups of settlers were moving inland to the west and north; and, in 1740, George II settled the boundary dispute with Massachusetts in New Hampshire's favor, adding townships and considerably increasing New Hampshire's area. By 1741, the province had solidified and prospered enough to support its own separate government.

The king now sought a governor for it who could be counted on to take good care of Britain's interests in lumber, naval stores, and—above all—mast pines for the navy. Benning Wentworth, son of the late lieutenant governor, was an ex-

1. Belknap, *History of N.H.*, 2:25.
2. May, *Early Portsmouth History*, p. 206.

cellent choice for his purposes and had, in fact, asked for the position of first governor. He received the appointment in 1741, remained in office for twenty-five years—the longest tenure of any governor of the colonial period—and was succeeded by his nephew, John Wentworth, who remained in power until the outbreak of the Revolution. "From an imperial point of view, the administration [of the Wentworths] operated as effectively as any in pre-revolutionary America." [3] By giving the province political continuity—notably lacking until 1717—the three Wentworths provided a uniquely stable government during the years leading to the Revolution. They also provided a style and tone that set a standard for life in Portsmouth and, indirectly, for the whole province. Like very few of their counterparts in the other colonies, they had been born in the area, and their lives had followed much the same pattern as those of their contemporaries and colleagues. They had risen to positions of wealth and power by way of business success in commerce; their marriages had never been disadvantageous; and their connections in England had been dependable and influential. It was a lucky combination for New Hampshire.

An effective colonial governor needed skill and patience to balance the mercantile interests of the mother country, on the one hand, and the changing demands of the settlers on the other. Leonard W. Labaree, in his study of the British Colonial system before 1783, suggests many areas in which the chain of command became unwieldy. It was almost impossible for the governor to control the legislative process in the king's interest, since the initiative for bills rested with the local assembly or council and he himself could only accept or reject what was proposed. Furthermore, many of the governor's powers could only be executed with the advice and consent of the council, and membership in that body—by appointment through the Board of Trade in England—was given to prominent and independent men of the provinces who, at least theoretically, held these positions for life. The governors, on the other hand, retained their

3. Jere R. Daniell, *Experiment in Republicanism* (Cambridge, Mass.: Harvard University Press, 1970), p. 5.

commissions only at the king's pleasure, and could be recalled for disobedience or inefficiency—terms that were open to widely divergent interpretations. Round trips to England with messages and directives took months, and deaths—of colonial officials and of kings and queens—frequently left a vacuum and disrupted the government. A constant vexation to all colonial governors was that their authority, in civil as well as military affairs, was limited by a lack of financial independence. One continuing source of dispute was the issuance of paper money. Benning Wentworth was severely censured for his reckless dependence on this expedient to alleviate New Hampshire's financial burdens.

Gradually, the self-confidence of the colonies grew and England—increasingly apprehensive—tightened the regulations and the system for overseeing the acts of the governors. There were always rival candidates willing to tell tales, and it was necessary to have friends at court who would see that the right counterinformation got into the right hands. There were infinite possibilities for the proffering and accepting of bribes when a position sought by two contestants was so far removed from England—geographically as well as ideologically. Operating successfully in this political thicket required agility of a rare sort.

For this particular type of transoceanic manipulation, Benning Wentworth had demonstrated outstanding skill. He had all the political tools he needed on both sides of the Atlantic, and he applied them in such a way that nobody felt unduly ill-used. However, an unvarnished account of his stewardship would be something of a shock to modern-day Americans. It was predicated on arrogant use of patronage and privilege, ruthless elimination of enemies, lavish nepotism in the interest of family and personal friends, and unbridled self-interest. Yet the machinations of this particular governor resulted in years of constructive growth for New Hampshire, which he cared for deeply, and insured the support of his king, for whom he had an abiding loyalty.

Benning Wentworth was bankrupt at the time of his appointment, but his friends in England were powerful, and they thought that he could be of signal service to the crown. They bailed him out financially and by obtaining his commission as governor assured him of a good salary funded on the local excise. In a very few years, he was one of the richest men in the province. This *tour de force* was achieved with a minimum of outrage from his constituents because, in almost every case, the people he used to further his ends also became rich and influential. Within his gift, as governor, were royal appointments, civil commissions, judicial and legislative offices, and military honors. These he distributed with care to guarantee the most useful and advantageous gratitude. One of his prerogatives was the disposal of hundreds of acres of ungranted land, which he used to charter 124 townships. The recipients were chosen, this time, to assure future delegates to the legislature who would favor the governor's plans.

Although the governor did require that some of his friends be included as proprietors of townships, that schools, the first settled minister, The Society for the Propagation of the Gospel and the Church of England be reserved for one share each; and that a large plot, usually 500 acres but sometimes as much as 800 acres be reserved for His Majesty's royal governor, not many complained.[4]

From those scarcely noticed acres of reserved land, Wentworth made his greatest financial killing. In 1743, he had also been appointed surveyor general of His Majesty's Woods and Forests at £800 a year, out of which he was to maintain four deputies. In letters to England describing his "valiant" battle to preserve the New England pines for the royal navy, he piously proposed that no new townships be established until the numbers and locations of mast pines had been recorded and that their preservation be a condition of tenure for future grantees. In reality, he

was describing his battle on behalf of himself and his fellow landowners to prevent claim-jumping woodsmen from felling timber and especially mast trees on the vast lands which had been enclosed. For the 'broad arrow' reservation applied on all his grants, as a means

4. Daniell, *Republicanism*, p. 16.

of insuring that he and his colleagues could dominate the lucrative mast trade.[5]

As more and more townships were settled to the north and west, new internal tensions began to appear. In theory, the governor's council was supposed to contain a balanced representation of up-country farmers and lumbermen and seaboard merchants, but in practice, distance and the vagaries of the weather militated against such a balance. Twelve of the thirteen members of Wentworth's council were Portsmouth residents. Furthermore, the governor's control over the entire court system was absolute. Despite the fact that all judicial appointments had been given to his friends and relatives, no one seriously complained—probably because these appointees, with few exceptions, were the best-educated and therefore the most qualified men for the bench. "Not only were judicial appointments made by Wentworth and the councilors, but together they acted without jury as a final court of appeals on matters both civil and criminal." [6] The situation in the superior, inferior, and probate courts was just as tightly controlled. Sometimes, by use of discreet influence, a privileged few could even obtain hearings out of court. Finally, the only courts in the province sat in Portsmouth. Aside from the fact that justice could hardly have been impartial under such conditions, the inconvenience of having to travel from frontier towns to receive it was viewed as an imposition by many. There was agitation, therefore, to break up the province into counties, with a court in each one. Wentworth and his council, for obvious reasons, opposed this move and were able to stave it off, but at some cost to his administration.

Seating of delegates to the House of Representatives also became a critical issue as the population of the state became increasingly diversified. In 1748, the House had only twenty members—eleven representing the four seacoast communities. All were elected in town meetings, but no one who owned real estate assessed at less than £300 was eligible, and the governor could issue election precepts to new townships at his own dis-

5. Malone, *Pine Trees and Politics*, p. 133.
6. Daniell, *Republicanism*, p. 19.

cretion. Wentworth could be sure that most people in the new inland settlements who qualified to vote were beholden to him, so he expected to control the delegates chosen by them. However, "As elected representatives they customarily felt more responsible to their local constituents than imperial interests, or the needs of the merchant aristocracy." [7] In general, Wentworth did not object to this situation, since it meant that the delegates would carefully attend to minor local issues that bored him. Such folk would seldom be in a position, he thought, to challenge his authority, and—even if they did—he alone had the power to convene, adjourn, prorogue, or dissolve the assembly at any time. He could also call for new elections, veto legislation, and negate the choice of speaker. His cavalier use of these powers and his stranglehold on the judicial system eventually created serious dissension. From 1748 to 1752—thanks to well-forged and carefully tended connections in England—Wentworth managed to survive and to fight off concerted attacks on his administration. It would be many years before even-handed representation for all towns would be a reality. In more general terms, however, it was perfectly clear during these years that the provincial assembly was thinking of itself more and more as the equal of the British Parliament, and therefore justified in challenging the prerogatives of a governor.

Not all Wentworth's energies and interests were expended on political ploys. Once his personal fortune had been recouped, he indulged and displayed his love of luxurious living with gusto. The result, for the province, was better than might have been expected. In company with friends and relatives, Wentworth helped to transform the bustling port town of Portsmouth into a provincial capital of style and grace. The prosperity of its inhabitants and the wealth of its merchants found particular expression in architecture, and the Wentworths and their wide family connections were responsible for building some of the most beautiful houses in America. The governor's own house, begun in 1749 on a magnificent site at Little Harbour, did not have the architectural purity of many of the others. John McClintock,

7. Daniell, *Republicanism*, p. 22.

writing in the nineteenth century, commented: "Where he obtained his plans, no one knows, but perhaps the irregularity of the structure was compensated by the grandeur and sumptuousness of its adornments." Its fifty-two rooms, tied together by "unlooked for steps and capricious little passages," were the product of successive additions.[8]

Over the years, through Wentworth's baronial gateway and along the stately driveways came shining coaches drawn by high-stepping horses, bearing the governor's friends, relatives, and political visitors. Sitting beneath Wentworth family portraits, on elegantly upholstered chairs, using the finest china and silver, Wentworth guests were served the best cuisine the province had to offer, complemented by wines imported from Europe. "The cellar [was] extensive, and for safety the governor kept his horses there in time of danger. A troop of thirty horses could here be accommodated." [9] After dinner, the guests could move to the billiard room, or to card rooms, to enjoy an ever-flowing punch bowl on the buffet, music from the spinet, and possibly dancing. To some in the province, the opulence of these parties and balls was an affront to traditional standards of public morality. The Congregational clergy, who resented Anglican domination of high provincial offices, were particularly critical of the high living in the governor's "court," on the ground that it was not a proper example for others.

A description of the governor's portrait hanging in Wentworth Hall "represents him dressed in the height of fashion, with a long flaxen peruke flowing in profuse curls to his shoulders. He has a handsome dignified face, the lips wearing an engaging smile and the air generally of face and figure of one who is 'lord of the manor'." [10] High living shows in his corpulent face and figure, and complacency informs every inch of his elegantly clothed person. He looks the very model of what he evidently enjoyed being—the leader of society in a provincial

8. John N. McClintock, *History of New Hampshire* (Boston: B. B. Russell, 1889), p. 191.

9. Charles W. Brewster, *Rambles About Portsmouth*, First Series (1873; facsimile edition, Somersworth, N.H.: New Hampshire Publishing Co., 1971), p. 102.

10. McClintock, *History of New Hampshire*, p. 191.

court. There is little doubt, either, that in the second half of the eighteenth century in Portsmouth, there were more than a few families whose wealth, sophistication, and pretentions enabled them to play to perfection the part of courtiers in Wentworth's ceremonious little kingdom.

According to a document written in 1750, however, conspicuous consumption was not the sole concern of New Hampshire's gentlemen of wealth.

> As the advancement of learning and the increase of all useful knowledge is of great importance both to the civil and religious welfare of a people, and as all gentlemen who have any taste for polite literature or desire to have any acquaintance with the various affairs of mankind—cannot but look upon it to be a great privilige to have always a good collection of books at hand . . . , it is therefore proposed to the gentlemen of this town, and a number of persons whose names are subscribed have agreed to join in purchasing a set of books to the value of about £12 for each man concerned, as the beginning of a library for their common use as a society.[11]

Although the governor himself was never accused of being bookish, several members of his family were listed as subscribers to this first attempt at a quasi-public library in Portsmouth. The first newspaper in the province, a weekly entitled the *New Hampshire Gazette,* came into being in 1756 in response to what its publisher sensed was encouragement from the townspeople of Portsmouth, and "depending upon the favor of all gentlemen who are friends to Learning, Religion and Liberty—so that I may go on cheerfully and continue this paper in a useful and entertaining manner."[12] Wentworth, conscious of the growing enthusiasm for culture and learning, authorized a gift of £300 from New Hampshire to Harvard College, where he had been educated. Unfortunately, however, he was instrumental in delaying the establishment of a center for higher learning in the province because he insisted that it be under the direction of the Bishop of London, while its supporters wished it to be independent.

11. May, *Portsmouth History,* pp. 223–224.
12. May, *Portsmouth History,* p. 226.

Despite his wealth and privileges, Wentworth suffered harsh personal problems. His family, like so many others at the time, was decimated by illness. His first wife and all three of their sons died while he was in office, leaving him, in 1759, a childless widower. By his second wife, who survived him by many years, he had two sons who died in infancy. "Throat distemper" (diphtheria) and yellow fever were terrifying and recurring scourges that took a heavy toll of the population, and the "constant communication with foreign places by sea, kept the town continually exposed to the small pox." As more became known about this disease, precautions were taken to prevent its spread. When a severe epidemic struck Boston in 1764, the regular stage service to Portsmouth was blocked by a fence built across the road. "A small house [was] erected to smoke all persons and baggage coming from Boston by land," and many wealthy residents went to Boston to be "carried safely through the disorder by inoculation." [13]

During King George's War (1744-1748), the capture of Louisburg, the French fortress at Cape Breton, added excitement and popular luster to Wentworth's governorship. Because England's long-drawn-out war with France had drained the energies and finances of the provinces that defended the northern frontier of America, the plan to attack the French at their own base appealed to all. Wentworth and the governor of Massachusetts authorized and funded the surprise attack to be commanded by William Pepperell, a popular Kittery merchant. According to plan,

> an army of volunteers were to quit their domestic connexions and employments, and engage in a hazardous enterprise. Professional skill and experience were entirely out of the question. Fidelity, resolution, and popularity must supply the place of military talents; and Pepperell was possessed of these. It was necessary that the men should know and love their General, or they would not enlist under him.[14]

By a series of fortuitous circumstances, the supposedly impregnable French fortress fell to the inexperienced American forces,

13. Adams, *Annals of Portsmouth*, pp. 187, 207.
14. Belknap, *History of N.H.*, 2:202-203.

but—to the rage and dismay of the men who had taken part—the prize was handed back to the French in the treaty of 1748.

By 1763, however, the final defeat of the French was a reality. In the years that followed, the autocratic control that Benning Wentworth had maintained for so long in the province began to break down. His chief agent in England, on whom his influence with the king had depended, began to fail physically and lose power. In the province, the mast trade, lumbering, and shipbuilding industries had gone into a serious decline, and the population in the interior and to the west was growing rapidly. All of these factors weakened the governorship and once Wentworth began to lose control over his constituents, his enemies exposed the tactics by which he had wielded his power. By 1766, the tide of public censure was overwhelming, and a resolution was drawn up to remove him from office. His nephew, John Wentworth, in England at the time, was able to negotiate a face-saving resignation for his uncle on grounds of ill-health. The final judgment on Benning Wentworth's governorship varies with the source, but in almost no account is it suggested that, for all his faults, he was other than a force that strengthened and steadied the province.

John Wentworth, who had prevailed upon the king to appoint him to succeed his uncle, was only thirty years old when he returned from England in 1767 to take up his duties. Arriving by land at the border of his province, he was met by several members of the council and a committee of the assembly escorted by a mounted troop. They were joined along the way by other citizens, and by the time the party reached Portsmouth, the whole formed "a grand cavalcade." Young Wentworth was taken in state to the council chamber, where his commission as governor and commander in chief of the province was read. He immediately directed all officers of the government to continue their duties, pending further order, and all present then retired for an "elegant entertainment." At the end of the day, a salute was fired, and the ships in the harbor displayed their colors. "Such ardency and emulation," concludes Nathaniel Adams in his account of the proceedings, "prevailed among all ranks on this occasion as gave the most promising hopes that his Excellency's government would be crowned with the most cordial affections of the people, whose happiness and his own were now so intimately blended." [15]

The extraordinary cordiality of John Wentworth's reception in Portsmouth probably would not have been duplicated everywhere in his domain. Approximately 52,000 people were then living in the province, which was roughly divided into three sections, comprising some ninety-eight towns. The seacoast towns, which paid two-thirds of the taxes, accounted for half the population; Portsmouth alone had 4,500 inhabitants. But in the Merrimack valley section, to the south, and the Connecticut valley frontier section to the west, the population was growing at a phenomenal rate. People from Massachusetts were settling the Merrimack area, and settlers from Connecticut were moving upriver to the frontier section. Most of these new settlers were farmers, although the distance from the coast forced them into limited manufacturing enterprises to supply local needs. These two sections, with little connection either geographically or ideologically with the seacoast, were also much more independent of England and the monarchy.

The young governor was more aware of the difficulties he would face in directing the affairs of New Hampshire than were his supporters on the seacoast. He understood that "the only order, peace, and obedience of the province [depended] on extending the power of government into the new settlements." [16] He was also willing to acknowledge defects in the workings of the imperial relationship, and he knew that he could no longer depend on the network of influence in England that had been enjoyed by his uncle. John Wentworth never questioned the premise that the mother country had the right to command her colony, but he recognized that the colonists' needs and feelings must be taken into account even as they were being required to support England. Given his age, background, experience, and wealth, the young governor's perspective was extraordinary. Unfortunately, this man—with his ideas, zeal, and commitment—would only serve New Hampshire for a total of eight years.

15. Adams, *Annals of Portsmouth*, pp. 222–223.
16. Daniell, *Republicanism*, p. 49.

John Wentworth's dedication to his responsibility as surveyor general of the woods was in direct contrast to his uncle's misuse of that position as a source of personal wealth. Determined to rectify the state of near anarchy that he knew existed in New Hampshire's lumber industry, young Wentworth had landed in South Carolina on his way home from England and had traveled up the coast through the other colonies to assess the "state of the woods." To complete his survey, he traveled extensively in the forests of his own territory, hoping to devise a way to supply masts for the king's navy without depriving the colonists of lumber for their mills. Wentworth won the respect of backwoodsmen and millmen by living their sort of life and listening to their point of view. Historian Joseph J. Malone has said that "he was the first royal official within their memories to travel so far and endure so many hardships in the performance of his duty." [17] During his travels, he acquired a sense of the geography of the province, and of the isolation of some of its settlements, and he noted differences in regional and sectional attitudes. Agricultural activity, which had been minimal near the coast, also was noted and supported by his special interest. He purchased a tract of land that had appealed to him in Wolfeboro on Lake Winnipesaukee and there established a large summer plantation where he conducted agricultural experiments and introduced new varieties of birds and fish. His experiences with the people who built his plantation house and worked for him there gave him a chance to appreciate the attitudes and interests of the inhabitants of the interior.

With the facts and insights thus acquired, and his early personal knowledge of Portsmouth and of the commercial potential along the seacoast, Wentworth decided on a course of action that would consolidate and strengthen the whole province. He proposed a system of roads, which would not only increase communication between isolated settlements but might also draw produce from all areas to the port of Portsmouth, thus providing an economic integration that would be mutually beneficial to the entire province. To decrease sectional rivalry and

17. Malone, *Pine Trees and Politics,* p. 138.

eliminate some of the inequities in the judicial system, he acceded to the long-needed division of the province into five counties, each with its own court. On the question of wider representation and a better-balanced House of Representatives, however, Wentworth felt he could not act because he feared a challenge to royal authority. He did see to it, however, that "several gentlemen of other respectable families, who had been treated with neglect in the preceding administration, were taken into favor; and a spirit of conciliation, among those who had formerly been at variance, seemed to mark the beginning of this administration." [18] The young governor was not in a position to influence the choice of delegates to the House, as his uncle had been, but he realized that the insistent demands of the inland towns for a voice in the government could not be forever ignored. He could, at least, and did enthusiastically support the founding of Dartmouth College in Hanover, for which he issued the charter in 1769.

As Lawrence Mayo emphasizes in *John Wentworth, Governor of New Hampshire,* he managed—by encouraging the expansion of foreign trade—to stabilize the financial situation in the province, gradually introducing gold and silver and abolishing paper currency. Mayo also points out that the governor strongly urged military preparedness. He even succeeded in reducing friction throughout a lumber industry caught between the demands of the royal navy and the growing needs of local communities. This result was achieved by judiciously looking the other way on some matters and holding firm on others. Wentworth and his wife were also active in social and cultural affairs. All in all, the governor might have expected that his administration would be long, popular, and constructive. But the Revolution took it all away from him and deprived New Hampshire of an outstanding statesman.

18. Belknap, *History of N.H.,* 2:345.

7

The Revolution

*A*S the revolt of the American colonies grew more immi-
nent, John Wentworth's position in New Hampshire was that of
a loving father trying to control a wayward child being led astray
by hotheaded friends. Wentworth never wavered in his convic-
tion that Parliament had the right to legislate for the colonies,
nor in his loyalty to the crown. He sincerely believed that armed
conflict could be avoided by forbearance on both sides. Pro-
ceeding with his plans for the province, he kept a calm paternal
demeanor and maintained a semblance of royal government as
usual. It is possible that he might have arbitrated matters so
skillfully that open rebellion could have been avoided, at least
for several years. But "antagonism to royal government
throughout the colonies inevitably weakened the ability of New
Hampshire provincial officials to command personal allegiance
and to maintain civil order." [1]

Historian Lawrence Mayo is of the opinion that, if the governor could have used his native guile and evenhandedness, he
probably could have lessened the violent reaction of the colonists to the Townshend Acts, which placed duties on various
commodities imported into America. As it was,

the popularity of the Governor of New Hampshire, and the influence of his numerous friends and connexions, who were of the prin-

1. Daniell, *Republicanism*, p. 52.

cipal families and the richest merchants in the Province, prevented the adoption of a non-importation agreement in Portsmouth till the merchants in some of the other Colonies threatened to withhold any mercantile intercourse with them.[2]

Wentworth had tried by every means to keep New Hampshire aloof from the rebellious attitudes of its neighbors, but unilateral behavior on the part of New Hampshire was impossible. In the inland portion of the province, the inhabitants were receiving news and pressure by way of Massachusetts and Connecticut from which he could not insulate them. By 1770, Exeter had become the center of disaffection for the more restless and impatient citizens.

The individual's reactions to the questions facing the colonies depended to a large degree on his personal situation, according to Richard F. Upton in his book, *Revolutionary America*. Upton classifies the inhabitants according to where they lived, what they did, what status they held, and what religious faith they professed. Each American colony, depending on its relationship with the mother country, had differing degrees of enthusiasm for the concept of armed rebellion; so, too, individuals within the colonies differed, on the same issues.

The geographical breakdown in New Hampshire began with the seacoast counties of Rockingham and Strafford, where the greatest wealth was concentrated along with the largest number of loyalists. Hillsborough, the middle county, on the other hand, had a radical population, with very few loyalists. Cheshire, the southern frontier county whose settlers had received royal land grants, was primarily royalist, while Grafton, much farther north, had no Tories at all.

By the time of the Revolution, the largest single bloc in New Hampshire was made up of farmers, a different sort of people from the seacoast settlers. The province never had had great areas of crop-producing land, but along the Connecticut River and in some central sections of the state, farming provided a fair living. The wealthier farmers were loyalists, but the rest—poor, proud, independent, and politically radical—opposed as oppres-

2. Belknap, *History of N.H.*, 2:346–347.

sive England's policies against issuing paper money. Insofar as they thought it through at all, they felt that they would be better off in an independent America. Throughout the province, laborers—mechanics, artisans, tradesmen, lumbermen, fishermen—formed the backbone of the "Sons of Liberty" and had a predilection for rioting. Joining them, but for different reasons, were the Congregational clergy, the best-educated men in New Hampshire, who had enormous influence over their congregations and who used their pulpits as platforms for political rhetoric. On the seacoast, the commercial class—merchants, shipbuilders, and financial enterprisers—was about evenly divided. In the interior of the state, however, this group provided the most influential and zealous leaders of the revolutionists, according to Upton. Professional men in general and lawyers in particular were initially opposed to the Revolution but later recognized that their chances of bettering themselves, financially and politically, probably lay in an independent America.

Obviously, the most devoted royalists, at the beginning, were the royal officials of the province based in Portsmouth—many of them beholden to the governor for their positions and directly responsible to the British government. In close relation to the distance from the seacoast, however, the lower county officials and militia officers tended to the radical view. Throughout the province, the judiciary was predominantly revolutionist in sympathy. Stated another way, those who had done well and had increased their wealth and influence wished to preserve the status quo. The emerging middle class across the state, consisting of able men restive under the exclusive political and social policies of John Wentworth and his seacoast oligarchy, provided the real backbone of the revolutionary movement. The poor and underprivileged, as always, welcomed a change on the general premise that anything would be an improvement.

Within the parishes of the province, there was wide divergence of view. Among the Quakers, opposed to war on principle, and the generally wealthy Episcopalians, whose ties with England discouraged revolutionary feelings, there was little enthusiasm for the struggle for independence. The Congregationalists, however, by far the largest body of believers, with 84 out of 118 churches in the province—espousing the doctrine of religious democracy and opposing the assumption of superiority by the Anglicans—provided the largest contingent of effective revolutionists. Some Presbyterian ministers of the Scotch-Irish churches also tended to be revolutionists.

In 1776, at the recommendation of the Continental Congress, a statement called the Association Test was circulated for signature among all white males over twenty-one in the American colonies. It read:

"We, the subscribers, do hereby solemnly engage, and promise that we will, to the utmost of our Power at the Risque of our Lives and Fortunes, with Arms, oppose the Hostile Proceedings of the British Fleets and Armies against the United American colonies." [3]

In New Hampshire, 16,000 men were eligible to receive it, and 9,348 of them were given the test. Many of the rest were by that time out of the state in various military capacities. Of those who took it, 8,567 signed. Upton estimates that only 646, or about seven percent, were actively opposed to the Revolution, while the rest were either indifferent and disinterested or genuinely in doubt as to the best course to follow. Although the ringing words of the Declaration of Independence were yet to be enunciated, New Hampshire colonists had long assumed the right to life and liberty, and their sense of personal independence was strong.

In the years immediately preceding the circulation of the Association Test, revolutionary sentiment had been rising, even in Portsmouth. A public meeting, held there in 1773 after the British attempt to tax tea, had adopted a preamble and eleven resolutions on American liberties. One resolution stated that union of all the colonies appeared to be the best guarantee of protection. This willingness to abrogate local independence in the interest of the larger common good acknowledged the possibility that collective action might have to be taken. The implications of such a statement, sent out with the preamble and other re-

3. Albert Stillman Batchellor, *Miscellaneous Revolutionary Documents of New Hampshire* (Manchester, N.H.: Printed for the State by the John B. Clarke Co., 1910), p. 2.

solves to all the towns in New Hampshire, can hardly have escaped notice. Statements of equal intensity were forthcoming from many New Hampshire towns. "Why the King's subjects in Great Britain should frame laws for his subjects in America, rather than the reverse," complained the Dover residents, "we cannot well conceive." [4]

In 1774, the Massachusetts Bay Colony was being punished for its violence over the tea tax, and from its citizens came steady agitation for action. By May, when the five Intolerable Acts were passed, Boston was at fever pitch. One of the five, the Boston Port Act, produced such an outcry when it was published in the *New Hampshire Gazette* that a Committee of Correspondence was formed. This committee dispatched a letter to Boston to express the sympathetic outrage of New Hampshire citizens, and "voted to give £200 for the relief of the industrious poor of the towns of Boston & Charlestown, under the oppression that they now suffer, from the port of Boston being blocked up by an act of the British Parliament." [5] The first meeting of the New Hampshire Assembly, which acted in open disobedience to the governor, was held at this time. When Wentworth tried to adjourn it, the members simply moved to another location and continued the session. One result of their deliberations was that a request was sent out to all the towns of the province for deputies to a convention in Exeter. This gathering was the first of a series of provincial conventions that sat in that town thenceforth till the end of the Revolution and out of which evolved the new state's system of governance. For the first convention, the most important business was choosing delegates from New Hampshire to go, at public expense, to the first Continental Congress in Philadelphia. Describing the need for such a meeting, Belknap may have coined the phrase used many years later by Winston Churchill as the title for his book about the period before World War II. Belknap said "To guard ourselves effectually against *the gathering storm* [italics mine], a union of the colonies was thought absolutely necessary; and

4. Daniell, *Republicanism*, p. 75.
5. Adams, *Annals of Portsmouth*, p. 245.

recourse was had to the same measure which had formerly been tried in cases of common danger, to hold a Congress of delegates from each colony." The Committee of Correspondence, which took charge of New Hampshire's actions at this time, also "recommended a day of fasting and prayer on account of the gloomy appearance of public affairs." [6]

Three specific events during the year 1774 in New Hampshire made even the most lukewarm revolutionists recognize the inevitability of the looming conflict. The first was Governor Wentworth's action in allowing New Hampshire carpenters to go to Boston to work on barracks for General Gage's British troops. This was his first serious misstep. The request for workers had been sent to the governors of all the neighboring provinces and Wentworth, increasingly torn by the conflicting demands of his role, hoped to comply without causing public outcry. Privately, he employed a person to hire men who lived near his Wolfeboro plantation, without telling them what their work was to be. The news soon got out, and he was publicly excoriated by the Committee of Portsmouth of which his uncle, Hunking Wentworth, was chairman. The second specific event that alarmed the settlers was the king's October edict forbidding the shipment of gunpowder to the colonies. And the third, announced by Paul Revere in a less-publicized ride on December 13, was that a British ship was on its way to reinforce the garrison at Fort William and Mary in Portsmouth.

Before the ship could arrive, a company of 400 New Hampshire patriots made a surprise raid on the fort, removed 100 barrels of powder, and confined the British officer and his men. The governor vociferously denounced this attack and ordered the immediate arrest of the perpetrators, but his authority had been badly weakened by his blunder with the carpenters, and the Committee of Portsmouth applauded rather than disapproved of the raid. When the British frigate *Scarborough* arrived in the harbor with a sloop and several companies of soldiers a few days later, all that remained in the fort were heavy cannon.

6. Belknap, *History of N.H.*, 2:370, 372.

From the first, the presence of the *Scarborough* caused resentment and conflict.

By 1775, even New Hampshire was a tinderbox. In January, another convention of the towns met at Exeter, issuing "an address to the people, warning them of their danger; exhorting them to union, peace and harmony, frugality, industry, manufactures and learning the military art; that they might be able, if necessary, to defend the country against invasion." [7] When, on April 19, General Gage's troops undertook what was intended to be a surprise attack to destroy the magazine of provisions and stores hidden in Concord, Massachusetts, they engaged in the first act of open warfare. By then, the men of New Hampshire were ready.

"Ready" is hardly the word, however, for the 1,200 ill-equipped and almost untrained zealots who marched that evening toward Boston. For many peacetime years, militia requirements, presumably in force statewide, had been only listlessly observed. Under the law, every male aged sixteen to sixty, had been expected to provide himself with a musket, bayonet, knapsack, cartridge box, one pound of powder, twenty bullets, and twelve flints. In each town, there was to be stored one barrel of powder, two hundred pounds of lead, and three hundred flints for every sixty men, besides a supply of all these for men unable to provide their own. All eligible males were supposed to appear for training; men over sixty were exempt from training, but were expected to have arms and ammunition. For several years Governor Wentworth, to his credit, had been urging the province to build up personnel and morale in the militia.

By the spring of 1775, when war became a real possibility, enthusiastic drilling of the volunteer militia in all the towns was undertaken. Because of the lax enforcement of the rules for supplies of arms and ammunition, however, very few men had even rudimentary equipment, and all had only makeshift uniforms. What they did have was spirit, determination, and a will

7. Belknap, *History of N.H.*, 2:378.

to fight that the British vastly underestimated. The most experienced men had been chosen for command, and the committees of correspondence in all the towns kept close watch on the situation. When the first alarm sounded, on April 19, the word spread rapidly from town to town, and in the next few days almost 10,000 New Hampshire volunteers streamed down in small companies to the outskirts of Boston.

Scenes of departure took place in every hamlet, village, and town. The following two accounts illustrate the spirit and gallant unreadiness of the rank and file of New Hampshire's inland revolutionists. The first took place in Peterborough.

> News of the Lexington battle fell upon them like a sudden trump from heaven summoning them to conflict. "We all set out," said one man, "with what weapons we could get, going like a flock of wild geese, we hardly knew why or whither." The word came to Capt. Thomas Morison at daylight, that the regulars were upon the road. In two hours, with his son and hired man, he was on his way to meet them, they on foot, he on horseback, with a large baking of bread, which had just been taken from the oven, in one end of the bag, and pork in the other.[8]

From a New Ipswich citizen came the comment: "In truth, that initial strife presented very little of what is sometimes called the 'glory of war.' In the provincial army, gorgeous uniforms, or in most cases any costumes that could receive such a name, were conspicuous by their absence." He went on to quote a fellow citizen's report on a departure from the town:

> To a man, they wore small-clothes, coming down and fastening just below the knee, and long stockings with cowhide shoes ornamented by large buckles, while not a pair of boots graced the company. The coats and waistcoats were loose and of huge dimensions, with colors as various as the barks of oak, sumach, and other trees of our hills could make them, and their shirts were all made of flax, and like every other part of the dress, were homespun. On their heads was worn a large round-top and broad-brimmed hat. Their arms were as various as their costume; here an old soldier carried a heavy Queen's arm—while by his side walked a stripling boy, with a

8. George Abbot Morison, *History of Peterborough, New Hampshire,* (Rindge, N.H.: Richard R. Smith Publishers, Inc., 1954), p. 480.

Spanish fusée not half its weight or calibre—while not a few had old French pieces—a large powderhorn was slung under the arm and occasionally a bayonet might be seen bristling in the ranks. Some of the swords of the officers had been made by our Province blacksmiths, perhaps from some farming utensil; they looked serviceable, but heavy and uncouth.[9]

In June 1775, it became obvious that a continental army under a commander in chief would have to be organized, and the New Hampshire legislature authorized a force of 2,000 men in three regiments to serve until December 31 to fulfill its quota in that army.

Even as the governor was attempting to defuse the situation, a New Hampshire convention in Exeter was sending an official letter to the Continental Congress in Philadelphia suggesting the assumption of permanent independence. This was the first specific allusion to independence in any known communication from anywhere in the country, and it was definitely at odds with Wentworth's constant reiteration that this was just a temporary problem that need cause no permanent break. From Philadelphia came communications stating that conciliation or compromise were no longer possible and that Parliament had voted the existence of rebellion in the new world.

On August 24, 1775, when it was no longer possible for him to pretend to run the government, Wentworth sailed off to Boston with his wife and child on the *Scarborough*. In September, he performed his last official act as royal governor. Traveling by chartered schooner to Gosport on the Isles of Shoals, within the provincial limits, he sent a secretary to the mainland with a proclamation proroguing the Assembly until April 1776. Then he left, never to return to the province he had tried so conscientiously to serve. A committee of Safety, appointed by the Provincial Convention took over the chief executive power in New Hampshire after the governor's departure. A committee of supplies was set up to tend to the needs of the army, and all official records and provincial funds (amounting to £1,516) were sent to Exeter for safety.

9. Charles Henry Chandler, *The History of New Ipswich* (Fitchburg, Mass.: Sentinel Printing Company, 1914), pp. 97–98.

At the opening of hostilities, the province faced three specific problems: the northern and western frontiers were susceptible to British and Indian raids from Canada; the seacoast and the great harbor of Portsmouth were exposed to raids from the sea; and New Hampshire had to supply and maintain men to defend these areas, as well as providing troops to fulfill its two-thousand-man quota for the Continental Army. Extensive preparations were made after General Washington sent Brigadier General Sullivan, a New Hampshire man, from Cambridge to command the local militia. An old ship was sunk at the mouth of the harbor to block incoming ships; fire rafts were constructed; riflemen were stationed on all points and promontories; lookouts were posted day and night. Three hundred men manned the forts in the harbor. The expense of these military necessities put a cruel burden on a none-too-affluent province. The problem of paying for the war for independence, as a matter of fact, was critical for all the colonies. Of them all, New Hampshire was the only one that never had to fight on its own soil during the Revolution. Although residents along the seacoast lived in constant fear of attack, and many people moved inland to avoid danger, no military action ever materialized there.

However, the men of New Hampshire fought bravely in every major battle from Bunker Hill to Yorktown, and some were even present at the evacuation of New York. Enoch Poor, James Reed, John Stark, Alexander Scammell, and John Sullivan, New Hampshire's outstanding officers, took their places with a score of others on the proud roster of the nation's Revolutionary heroes. The total number of enlistments in New Hampshire regiments from 1775 to 1783 is estimated at almost 18,500, though it must be noted that this figure includes re-enlistments. No exact tally of all the dead can be made, but according to J. Duane Squires, in his recent history of the state, "In the Granite State of the mid-twentieth century upwards of 4,500 Revolutionary war soldier graves had been identified and many of them appropriately marked." [10] Many more soldiers must

10. J. Duane Squires, *The Granite State of the United States*, 4 vols. (New York: American History Company, Inc., 1956), 1:134.

have been buried where they fell, and some died of disease on the ill-fated expedition to Quebec and elsewhere. At the Battle of Bunker Hill alone, 107 of the 911 New Hampshire volunteers were either killed or wounded. In the last months of the New England campaign, the special guerilla skills that New Hampshire men had learned at such cost in the protracted French and Indian wars were especially effective against British soldiers, in no way prepared to fight in the American wilderness. New Hampshire men also served with valor at sea, both in the newly formed navy and on privateers—many owned and operated by Portsmouth citizens.

8

The Constitution

URING July 1776, in every shire town of New Hampshire, the beating of drums brought the populace into the streets to hear the great news. The American colonies had officially declared their independence. In Portsmouth, it was proclaimed on July 18 and "was received in this town with lively expressions of joy, notwithstanding their former votes." [1] Belknap wrote of the Declaration:

> It relieved us from a state of embarrassment. We then knew the ground on which we stood, and from that time everything assumed a new appearance. . . . The single question was, whether we should be conquered provinces or free and independent states. On this question every person was able to form his own judgment; and it was of such magnitude that no man could be at a loss to stake his life on its decision. [2]

In a fever of revolutionary spirit, some townspeople tore down street signs named after a king or queen, threw rocks at signboards displaying symbols of royal power, and refused to accept the halfpence in business transactions because it bore the name of George III. No noisy demonstrations attended the public reading of the letter brought by express to Exeter on July 18.

1. Adams, *Annals of Portsmouth*, p. 263.
2. Belknap, *History of N.H.*, 2:405.

News of its arrival had flown around town, and every man, woman, and child dropped his work and hastened to the center to hear the long-hoped-for news. The document was read aloud, the reader overcome with emotion from time to time. Sober joy was the reaction.

What the more sophisticated and better-educated colonists recognized was that "the Revolution had not only involved the colonies in war, but had thrust upon them the perils of self-government." [3] For New Hampshire the experience may not have been as traumatic as it was for some of the other colonies. Throughout the province's history, the settlers from time to time had had to "go it alone," and in each challenging and dangerous situation it had become evident that collective debate and action was the only way to proceed. All the towns of the province, while differing widely in social make-up and source of livelihood, agreed on one supreme principle: they wanted to be allowed to run their own affairs. Most of them had learned, however, that it was more profitable and safer to do so in conjunction with other towns. Therefore, by the time the idea of a larger unit of union—America—began to be circulated for their recommendation and vote, they were ready to entertain the concepts of a federal Constitution, a Bill of Rights for all Americans, an over-all financial system, and, as a first step, a Continental Navy and a Continental Army to carry on the war.

The three New Hampshire regiments under Stark, Reed, and Poor were melded without difficulty into the Continental Army, and thenceforth were subject to battle orders from the new commander-in-chief, George Washington. The Continental Congress at this time took an important step toward collective action by forbidding the export of goods needed in America. The sudden dearth of British supplies had created serious shortages, and more attention had to be paid to distribution of needed items among colonies and provinces. It was also necessary to begin thinking of each other as allies with common problems, rather than as separate entities with dissimilar goals, connected with and dependent upon Great Britain.

3. McClintock, *History of New Hampshire*, p. 401.

Three weeks before publication of the Declaration of Independence, New Hampshire had instructed "our delegates in the Continental Congress to join with the other colonies in declaring the thirteen United Colonies a Free and Independent State; solemnly pledging our faith and honor that we will on our parts support the measure with our Lives and Fortunes." [4] The New Hampshire signers of the Declaration were William Whipple, Matthew Thornton, and Josiah Bartlett. The province became officially the state of New Hampshire on September 11, 1776, and its chief executive was to be called its president. When the title was changed to governor, in 1793, Josiah Bartlett was in office and thus became the state's first executive officer to be called *governor*, though he was not its first president.

On January 5, 1776, the Fifth Provincial Congress of New Hampshire, meeting in Exeter, formed itself into a House of Representatives and created a second legislative body called the Council. The House consisted of eighty-nine representatives from the five counties, representation from each based on its population. The House chose twelve men for the Council. New Hampshire thus became the first of the thirteen colonies to set up a state government. Its architects, however, insisted that this action was not to be viewed as the work of hotheaded revolutionists, but as the prudent provision of responsible men for the period after Wentworth's departure until the end of the war, when the old ties with Britain would be enthusiastically resumed. Not everyone viewed it that way, nor wished to, but for the duration of the "dispute," the necessity for a state constitution was acknowledged by all. Many must have recognized that the step was irrevocable. Once all taxpayers had been given the franchise and each town had been authorized to elect its own representatives—on the basis of ability rather than on ownership of real estate—the growing middle class, with its strong revolutionary bias, had its toe in the door.

The governmental structure of the state as adopted had serious flaws, notably the lack of an executive branch. However, the Committee of Safety, which had been authorized by an

---

4. McClintock, *History of New Hampshire*, p. 376.

earlier provincial convention in Exeter during the hectic days following Wentworth's departure in 1775, had been given wide executive powers and was able to fill the gap. This powerful group, consisting of six to sixteen men drawn from among the most able in the state, was appointed annually. Over the war years, forty-three men served on it. Its chairman was president of the Council. In 1776, Colonel Meshech Weare was chosen to assume this dual role and also to serve as Chief Justice of the Superior Court of New Hampshire. He held these three offices until 1784, when he was elected president of the state of New Hampshire. His abilities, wisdom, and strength of character were in large part responsible for New Hampshire's emergence as a powerful national force.

One of the first acts of the new legislature in 1776 was to establish a judicial system. The court of appeals was abolished to eliminate the possibility of appeals to Great Britain. Two steps were then taken to insure that law and order would continue to be preserved. The imaginative first one illustrates how much the leaders of New Hampshire had learned from the province's experience with uncertain jurisdictions under the Mason Grants and sporadic control by the Massachusetts Bay Colony. All the laws on the books were examined and those that were no longer relevant were eliminated. The others were readopted to make sure that they would remain in effect through the switch from royal province to independent state. The second step was to pass several new laws and regulations required either because of the war or as a result of the traumatic break with England. Among those pertaining to the war were a reorganization of the militia and several regulations affecting trade and privateering.

The office of maritime officer was established at Portsmouth to enforce and oversee all trade regulations. Every ship in and out had to be cleared and her cargo and destination declared. The Continental Congress requisitioned supplies of rum and beef in New Hampshire in accordance with the system whereby all the states were called upon to provide commodities for the whole. From 1775 to 1783, privateering consumed the energies of a great many people in Portsmouth—so many that the recruitment of seamen for the newly established Continental Navy was seriously prejudiced. Privateers were required to have congressional authorization, and their captured prizes were brought into port to be libeled, tried, usually condemned, and sold at auction. In 1776, an admiralty or maritime court was established at Portsmouth for this purpose, and William Saltonstall estimates that, for the next six years, almost one hundred privateers went in and out, preying on British shipping. These ships, armed and heavily manned, made handsome fortunes for their owners and crews. One Portsmouth resident who profited from the privateering business in an unusual way was the man who auctioned off the captured English vessels. He was able to build one of the handsomest brick houses in town (perhaps designed by Bulfinch), with the money thus earned.

"The war in which we became involved with Britain, found us not destitute of resources, but unskilled in the art of finance," [5] wrote Jeremy Belknap, who was living during the period and was therefore in a position to observe the financial chaos that plagued New Hampshire. Until the Revolution, Britain had redeemed paper currency and reimbursed and sustained New Hampshire's trade. Now, however, all the former provinces and colonies were on their own, faced with an expensive war they were not at all sure of winning, and lacking a unified financial system. In New Hampshire, where every day of war increased the state's debts, the easy solution seemed to be paper money. Violence and trickery were used to pressure the legislature to issue it, but the wise recognized that in that direction lay further disaster. Because silver and gold were gradually being siphoned off to pay for imports from other countries, many transactions had to be carried out in goods. Taxation on polls and property—the usual expedient adopted by the House of Representatives, which had the authority for the state's finances—was hard on the husbandmen and laborers whose incomes were scanty or nonexistent. Loan offices were tried, and a variety of laws were passed, only to be repealed later on in a frantic attempt to regulate matters. Counterfeiters were prevalent, and a law to punish their activities was passed. When the

5. Belknap, *History of N.H.*, 2:425.

House recommended the confiscation and sale of the personal estates of people who had quit the state—directing the proceeds into Continental loan certificates—so much resentment, resistance, and legal confusion resulted that the net monetary return was negligible. Endless meetings and discussions and conventions with other New England states were held, but sound fiscal policies and debt reduction programs did not become a reality in America until after the war, when a federal system of regulation was adopted.

Besides actively prosecuting a war, defending vulnerable boundaries, devising a workable system of government within a state constitution, and trying to prevent the total collapse of state finances, New Hampshire's leaders faced a problem peculiarly their own in the western part of the state bordering the Connecticut River. About a hundred towns formed under charters received from Governor Benning Wentworth, and known for years as the New Hampshire Grants, lay on the west bank of the river. Their inhabitants had bitterly resented the king's 1764 decision that the river should form the boundary between New York and New Hampshire. They had wanted either to join the settlers on the east bank of the river in New Hampshire, with whom they had far more in common than with the inhabitants of New York, or to stand alone as a separate state. In the end they chose independence, as the state of Vermont. Thirty-six New Hampshire towns on the east bank of the river, dissatisfied with the state constitution adopted in Exeter in 1776 on several important issues, including representation, property qualifications, and civil rights, temporarily seceded and joined Vermont, which had declared its independence in July 1777. The Revolution had brought the Connecticut River valley into sharp focus, and the threat was a dangerous one. It was, in fact, a question of possible civil war, and the loss of valuable townships in the fertile river plain.

The alienation of the western communities, and the possibility that they might permanently secede from New Hampshire, demanded the attention of New Hampshire's leaders at a time when they were harried by other concerns.

The New Hampshire state constitution in effect today became

operative July 1, 1784. It took shape during five years of debate and controversy, in a democratic process that was slow but sound. The original draft, adopted in 1776, had come under increasing fire, particularly from the western part of the state. Between 1778 and 1784, it had been given three major revisions before the requisite two-thirds majority of the voters agreed to approve it. With patience and care and attention to the will of the people as expressed through town meetings and plebiscites, the legislators had dedicated themselves to providing an acceptable state constitution. At times—as their representatives returned to the people again and again with a new draft, only to have it rejected—ratification must have seemed an almost impossible goal.

Voters in the western part of the state had been the most intransigent. A majority of them had come from Connecticut, where they had already been exposed to democratic forms of government. They had learned to distrust a strong central government run by men whose interests were primarily those of the seacoast, and who were not willing to give fair representation in councils of state to every area. They hotly resented property qualifications for voters and representatives, and their pressure helped to reduce considerably—though not to eliminate—such qualifications. After the war, when the revised civil constitution for the state was adopted, representation from these towns was equalized, and—with the removal of the capital to Concord in 1807—their inhabitants began to feel truly a part of the state. The threat of secession by the thirty-six western towns forced state leaders to recognize the town as the political unit of representation in the legislature. Because of this, New Hampshire today has the largest House of Representatives in the United States—an unwieldy and expensive body of more than 400 members.

Every town was given the right to tax its residents for the maintenance of social services and to choose its own officers. The selectmen—three to five elected annually for each town— were, from the beginning, called "Fathers" of the town. Underlying the political structure of the state government were two main principles. The first, at the local level, was what the thirteen colonies, at the national level, had fought the Revolution to achieve: it held that the people should have sole and exclusive right to govern themselves in a free, sovereign, and independent state or nation. The second was that the three essential powers of the government—legislative, executive, and judiciary—should function as independently of each other as possible.

A sturdy Bill of Rights was prefixed to the constitutional document. Although twenty-three of its thirty-eight articles were copied verbatim from the Massachusetts constitution of 1780, the insistence on the importance of human rights by the rank and file of New Hampshire people throughout the state was overwhelming. No state constitution written without due regard for their convictions on such matters could ever have been approved. Because of these thirty-eight articles, the New Hampshire resident of 1784 felt that he was assured of his personal freedom, the security of his property, and the peace and order of the society in which he was to live. He was then—and only then—willing to take the following oath of fidelity to the state:

> I do truly and sincerely acknowledge, profess, testify and declare that the State of New Hampshire is and of right ought to be a free, sovereign and independent State; and do swear that I will bear faith and true allegiance to the same; and that I will endeavor to defend it against all treacherous conspiracies and hostile attempts whatever. . . . So help me God.[6]

The seal of state that was adopted at this time featured a border of laurel surrounding a field on which was displayed a ship under construction flying the American colors. In the background is a felled pine tree against a sun rising from the ocean. The Latin words *Sigillum Reipublicae Neo Hantouiensis* once ringed it, but it now bears the English translation, "Seal of the State of New Hampshire, 1776." Although in 1784, when the constitution was adopted, a wise provision was made to call a convention in seven years to consider any revisions of the government that might be needed, changes over the years have been minor. The skill, wisdom, and patience of such men as Josiah Bartlett, Meshech Weare, John Sullivan, John Langdon, and

6. Belknap, *History of N.H.*, 3:271.

many others who helped to fashion a state out of what was a loosely defined and disconnected province, must impress us still.

While the citizens of the thirteen states were hammering out their constitutions, trying to function socially and economically, and doing their part on the Revolution's battlefields, men in Philadelphia were trying to do the same thing for the emerging union of states. The concept "United we stand, divided we fall" that recommended itself so strongly to the various towns within states, could and did make even more urgent sense at the national level.

If, as men adjusted to independence in New Hampshire, it had been increasingly evident that systems of control—of trade regulations, or currencies—in the state could not be effective if they were not tied in with those of at least the neighboring states, so in an even more vital way did confederation of the states seem the only expedient for the country. After initial recognition in 1775 of the need for a centrally ordered military establishment to win the war, the Continental Congress had called on each state for men and material on a quota basis. Once this practical military necessity for united action had been accepted, it was possible to move on to more abstract mutual concerns. It soon became obvious that all the states should share in designing a federal constitution for the new nation.

From the meeting of the First Continental Congress in 1774 to the end of the war, fourteen different men from New Hampshire served on national bodies. What they were learning in their own state was put to good use in the national debate. Although the journey to the seat of the national government—moved several times during the war—was arduous, and lodgings during prolonged sessions of Congress were expensive, the New Hampshire delegates were remarkably faithful.

During the early sessions, sectional rivalries and state pride sometimes hindered progress, but by November 1777, Articles of Confederation were approved by the Congress and ready for consideration by the thirteen state governments. Brought to New Hampshire just before Christmas, they were at once dispatched throughout the state—despite snow and ice—to be voted on in the towns. By March 1778, returns favoring acceptance were in, and the Articles were formally ratified by the New Hampshire legislature. Once again, Josiah Bartlett set his name to a historical document for New Hampshire. However, the Articles were not to go into effect for almost three years—until the unanimous approval of all the states had been sought and obtained.

In November 1782, the provisional peace treaty between the United States and Great Britain was signed in Paris. The Continental Congress received word of the signing the following March, and at once sent dispatches with the good news to every state. Ratification of the final treaty draft by the Congress was not accomplished until January 1784, but to the people of New Hampshire, the war ended with the receipt of the dispatch from the Continental Congress in March 1783. They celebrated on April 28—a day of public Thanksgiving proclaimed by the Committee of Safety. Real work lay ahead; war debts were pressing; independence would bring painful realities. But for that one day, at least, the mood throughout the state was one of celebration and joy.

By 1787, the states had discovered that, although the Articles of Confederation had been a start, they proved, in practice, not to be adequate. Once again, therefore, the states were asked to send delegates to Philadelphia—this time to make revisions. John Langdon and Nicholas Gilman, authorized New Hampshire deputies, arrived late, but forcefully advocated a strong central government that would pay particular attention to commercial regulations, national defense, and taxation. Langdon, a distinguished and wealthy public figure at the age of forty-six, paid travel expenses for both himself and Gilman.

When the two men returned jubilantly to New Hampshire with the proposed Federal Constitution (which needed the approval of only nine states for ratification), they were surprised to find that considerable opposition to it had developed in the convention sitting in Exeter to vote on it. Assembled were 112 delegates from 175 towns. Consideration of the Constitution was to be no hasty matter, for despite the fact that six states had already ratified it, the men of New Hampshire demanded time to go over it word by word. When it became obvious during these deliberations that opposition was alarmingly strong, convention leaders secured enough votes for adjournment and a motion to reconvene in Concord on June 18.

There, the vote was finally put to the delegates on June 21, 1788. "Whilst the Secretary was calling over the members, and recording their votes," wrote Nathaniel Adams, "a death-like silence prevailed; every bosom throbbed with anxious expectation." [7] The count was close—fifty-seven yeas to forty-six nays—but it was enough. New Hampshire had the distinction of casting the ninth and therefore the deciding vote that put the Constitution into effect—two other states having ratified during the four-month New Hampshire adjournment. Twelve proposed citizens' rights amendments to the Constitution recommended for adoption were included in the report of the New Hampshire convention—a recognition of the feelings of some "nay" voters who had objected to their absence in the Constitution as voted.

Following the adoption of the Constitution, the next step was to elect the first president of the United States. New Hampshire was entitled to five electors. At a session of the Congress on April 6, 1789, in New York City, John Langdon, then president of the U.S. Senate, counted the votes that unanimously gave the presidency and vice-presidency of the new nation to George Washington and John Adams. The first U.S. senators elected from New Hampshire were John Langdon and Paine Wingate; the first members of the House of Representatives were Nicholas Gilman, Samuel Livermore, and Abiel Foster.

New Hampshire was fortunate that, during those turbulent, all-important years, men of caliber appeared from all over the state to provide the combination of talents needed to lead New Hampshire into statehood, and to allow her to join with pride in the formation of the United States. It was a feature of the times that a man's education—or lack of it—and his profession or means of livelihood in no way restricted his political activities. So it was that, of the six most prominent New Hampshire politicians of the revolutionary period, three had had very little formal education. John Langdon and Nicholas Gilman had at-

7. Adams, *Annals of Portsmouth*, p. 290.

tended only the common schools, and Josiah Bartlett, although he was a practicing physician, had had only a minimum of training other than observation. John Sullivan had studied law and been trained for the army; Paine Wingate, a clergyman, was a Harvard graduate; and Meshech Weare had a Harvard degree in law.

Early in life, these men had earned public confidence and proven capability in their chosen fields, and it occurred to no one to question their credentials for public service. If a man proved that he was astute, useful, and upright in one form of endeavor, the assumption was that he could apply himself equally in another. Training for public office was entirely on the job, and men of outstanding ability, once "discovered," were elected to several unrelated offices at the same time, and then re-elected—over and over again. Dr. Josiah Bartlett, a physician by inclination, served for many years as chief justice of the state, was many times sent as New Hampshire's representative to national conventions, where he served on the most important and diverse committees; and was frequently called upon to officiate as a justice of the peace. Weare, Langdon, Sullivan, and Bartlett all served for years in an incredible variety of posts, and were repeatedly honored by election to one-year terms as president—and, when the nomenclature was changed in 1793, as governor of the state.

Part II

State

9

A Way of Life

*T*HE detailed working specifications for what life was like in the state of New Hampshire in the opening years of the nineteenth century had been clearly stated some years before by the principal author of the Declaration of Independence. In 1781, in reply to a question from Barbé de Marbois, the secretary of the French legation in Philadelphia, Thomas Jefferson said:

> Those who labor in the earth are the chosen people of God, if ever He had a chosen people, whose breasts He has made His peculiar deposit for substantial and genuine virtue. It is the focus in which He keeps alive the sacred fire which otherwise might escape from the face of the earth. Corruption of morals in the mass of cultivators is a phenomenon of which no age nor nation has furnished an example. It is the mark set on those who, not looking up to heaven, to their own soil and industry, as does the husbandman, for their subsistence, depend for it on casualties and caprice of customers. . . . Generally speaking, the proportion which the aggregate of the other classes of citizens bears in any state to that of the husbandmen is the proportion of its unsound to its healthy parts and is a good enough barometer whereby to measure its degree of corruption. While we have land to labor, then, let us never wish to see our citizens occupied at a workbench or twirling a distaff. Carpenters, masons, smiths are wanting in husbandry, but, for the general operations of manufacture, let our workshops remain in Europe.[1]

1. Bernard Mayo, editor, *Jefferson Himself* (Boston: Houghton Mifflin Company, 1942), pp. 34–35.

Throughout the ensuing years, Thomas Jefferson elaborated and refined these propositions. Schemes for industry, banks, cities were all sources of possible—indeed probable—evil; they were engines designed to condense or explode the fortunes of individuals, aliments for all sorts of popular rages. In sum, Jefferson was convinced that "the true foundation of republican government is the equal right of every citizen in his person and property and in their management," and he was sure that such a foundation could best be secured by men who owned and worked their own land—farmers, the chosen people.[2] When he was inaugurated as president of the United States in 1801, he took these ideas along with him.

For the better part of the first half of the nineteenth century, these ideas acted as a leaven in the Jeffersonian constituency that became in time the Democratic party. And during that period, the Democratic party and the Jeffersonian vision were the governing influences in the life of the state of New Hampshire.

As the century opened, the conditions prescribed by the ideal were imposed on the citizens by simple necessity. In 1800, there were 183,858 people living within the state's boundaries. They were dispersed among 219 towns and villages. Of these settlements, 137 were communities that numbered less than a thousand souls. In the state there was no city, and one bank was situated in the largest town, Portsmouth (population 5,339), on the seacoast. Nowhere was there what was later called a manufactory, which then meant a small water-powered textile mill. Within the next ten years, twelve of these establishments were built, but their effect on the total economy was insignificant. As the *Gazetteer of the State of New Hampshire* said in 1823, "New Hampshire is emphatically an agricultural state." The number engaged in commerce, which—save in Portsmouth—meant tending the village stores, was 1,068. In manufactures, there were 8,699, most of them working in the 801 grain mills and 1,148 sawmills scattered about the state. The number of persons in agriculture was 52,384. The citizens, it was said, did

2. Mayo, *Jefferson*, p. 323.

not wish to create "extensive manufactories in which must be required large capitals, and a patience and automaton constancy to which we are unused." Thus the intent was to make "comparatively little for exportation" except for surplus farm produce. Still, it was obvious that "to be independent we must manufacture for ourselves," so "in the departments of *domestic* and *household* manufactures our citizens already excel." More cloth and shoes were made at home in those days than were made in factories or brought in from beyond the borders.[3]

This was a society, shifting away from coastal conditions, in which almost all the members lived close to the land, fixed within the timeless chores of farming. One farm, one town, one day was much like another. Elements to produce change and differentiation were introduced early in the nineteenth century, but for a long period did not acquire sufficient energy to work very significantly against the prevailing shape of things. Even the population remained fairly constant—from 1800 to 1860, New Hampshire grew at an average rate of 10 percent each decade. Through the same period, the country as a whole increased by 34 percent every ten years. And the average figure for the state concealed, as averages sometimes do, a clear tendency. At each census, it was revealed that men and women in increasing numbers were leaving the state and that the rate of growth was slowing down. By 1860, when there were 2 percent more people than there had been in 1850, it was clear that the society was approaching the steady state. It seemed, as is frequently said of the whole world today, that New Hampshire was then reaching the limits of growth imposed by conditions of nature.

Agrarian, self-sufficient, stable—it was also, in the Jeffersonian definition, a place of "substantial and genuine virtue." What, in that situation, was life like? To begin with, it was a life of very hard work. Those who set out to manage their own persons and property had to spend most of their time doing it. For one thing, there was the terrain. Along the Connecticut

3. John Farmer and Jacob B. Moore, *A Gazetteer of the State of New Hampshire* (Concord, N.H.: J. B. Moore, 1823), pp. 7–29.

River, there was a narrow band of land that was not only lovely to look upon but was also excellent for growing things. And in the interior, the soil around some of the river bottoms was good. But for the most part, as travellers so often said, there were more hills than dales and the ground was rocky, thin, and acid. Then there was the relentless drama of the weather that cut down sharply at both ends of the growing season. To start a farm, as some did, in the early days in the North Country around Lancaster, took more fortitude, in the opinion of Yale College president Timothy Dwight, than to settle a whole empire.

For the working of this land there were hand tools—hoes, forks, axes, mattocks, flails, and rakes that had come down from numberless earlier generations. It took a long time to mow an acre of standing grass with a scythe, to cut a cord of wood with an axe, to build a stone wall with a bar and perhaps a gin pole. Horses, and in the early days, more often oxen, were the prime movers for heavy loads and sometimes they worked the small treadmills. But for the rest, in reaping, hewing, shearing, lifting, sawing, pitching on, digging out, the energy came from human backs, legs, and shoulders. The men in New Hampshire in those days earned their bread, whether it was ninety degrees in the shade or twenty degrees below zero, just as men before them had for a thousand years. No one, 150 years later, with a chain saw in his hand, or at the throttle of the spray rig in the helicopter, or sitting in the air conditioned cabin of a tractor listening to music on the radio, can quite imagine what farm work was like in those days.

Insofar as liberation is a function of equality, the women were liberated: they worked just as hard as the men—and somewhat longer. The average membership in the family in the first part of the last century was 6.7, and mothers did most of the things necessary to feed and clothe that membership. They often tended the garden; invariably processed, one way and another, all the foodstuffs; often picked and cleaned the wool; usually spun and wove and cut and sewed. They washed, scrubbed, mended, fed the young stock, raked scatterings in the haying season, administered herbal teas to the feverish, picked apples in the fall, bore 4.7 children and—especially in the first two decades—brought in a good deal of the family cash. The money came from the butter they made and stored in the cold cellars and from the wool, brought to them by agents, that they spun at their wheels by the fireside. Once a year, a good many women rode, like Betsy Robbe, sixty miles and more to Boston, with two fifty-pound tubs of butter slung in bags over a horse's back to sell their produce in the market.

Filled as was their present with the endless details of the day's work, these women often also thought of better futures for their children and tried to do something about that. When Mrs. Robert Wilson rode to Boston twice a year, she led a pack horse laden with butter and linen she had made from flax she had grown. When these goods had been sold, she rode on to Andover to pay the bursar for the food, tuition, and books used in her son's education at Phillips Academy. A good many boys, in these years, went off to academies in Chesterfield, Amherst, New Ipswich, or Exeter because their mothers set store by a learning they did not have, themselves, and made that learning possible. And many of these sons, once started, went on to Harvard or Dartmouth.

For men and women and boys and girls on farms, work meant, most obviously, physical exertion. But, especially for the men, it meant also incessant practice in the arts of negotiation. In a state with few banks and less money, the way ends were made to meet and things were put together was, often, by trade, borrow, and swap. A farmer would take three dollars, six bushels of turnips, and five calves to a neighbor. The neighbor would keep the money and the vegetables and kill and dress the calves. He would return the dressed meat and four skins to the farmer, keeping one for himself. The farmer would take the skins to another neighbor, who would tan them for something less than a dollar and a half-bushel of wheat. And then another man would come for three days to the farmer's house to make five pairs of shoes and a pair of pumps out of the calfskin. The following week, the farmer would go for a day to the house of the man who had made the shoes, to make an ox yoke and two whiffletrees for the hay-cart.

This was the way it went in all things great and small. When a man wanted to build a house, he sought out a neighbor like Oliver Holmes. He supplied all the materials Holmes needed and gave him and two boys board, but not room, for eight months. When the house was finished, in June, he gave him, as agreed the previous November, one hundred dollars and a two-year-old heifer.

At the time Oliver Holmes had the house frame ready for raising, more labor was needed to do the job, so people came to help from several miles around. At the end, the owner of the new house cooked about forty pounds of beef, "flour bread," Chinese tea, and fed forty men and boys. When labor more continuous was needed, more formal deals were made. Thomas Eaton of Francestown agreed in 1802 to take the son of Daniel Wilkins of Amherst to live with him until the boy was twenty-one years old. If the boy did well, it was agreed, he would, at the end of the period, get one hundred dollars and two suits of clothes. All this was agreed to within the hearing of three witnesses.[4]

Between the work and the negotiation, close to the ground and near to the neighbors, the time was spent, almost all of it, in keeping body and soul together, making, as it used to mean, one's own living. Entries in diaries and day books indicate how the days were worked out in careful calculations and measurements. A man would record the fact that he killed a sow that weighed eight score pounds, that he took seventeen hay loads off the lower meadow, that he settled a debt with his neighbor for two oak logs of seventy-six feet, that his wife died last night at the age of fifty-eight years, two weeks, and two days, that he bought at the store a pint of rum, a pound of snuff, and one ounce of wafers.

David Clark, who spent his early years among men who made such calculations before he went off to start a singing school and to read in a desultory fashion in the law, suggested in his diary some of the difficulties of giving proper interpretation to such evidence. When sailors record dangers in the upper

4. Diaries and Cash Book of Thomas Eaton, Dartmouth College Manuscript Collections, Hanover, N.H.

regions in their log books, or lawyers speak of sovereign decisions of judges, or doctors mention the power of new medicines, he said, people are greatly impressed. But there is only amused condescension when farmers soberly note down that the crop of hay was not as great as last year nor was as much as was expected a month since and that there have been no rains this three weeks of any consequence before yesterday's.

And indeed it is hard to know with any certainty what may be behind and beyond this kind of testimony. In what way may all these precisely quantified small transactions be taken as the saving works of a chosen people? No one living after the event can ever accurately gauge the quality of the event as it took place. Are the last enchantments of the Middle Ages to be discovered in the sparse routines of Girth the Swineherd or to be deduced from Blondel's songs? Fortunately, in this difficult matter, suggestive evidence of various kinds does exist.

Take the memory of a man who grew up on a farm during the first third of the century. Looking back some years later, he said:

> Two or three hundred acres of forest had been brought into conditions of a well ordered farm with a due proportion of arable fields, meadows, pastures, orchards and woodlands. Several miles of stone walls had been built and the large barns were shifted to the ridge pole with hay and grain. Every stanchion was filled with cattle tied up for the winter and the stable with horses and a huge pen grunted with swine. One cellar was filled from the ground to the ceiling with potatoes, another with hogs heads of cider, leaving scarcely room for the apple bins, much frequented by boys and girls going to school. Another was appropriated for the use of the dairy, which occupied all the women in the house. And the cheese safe contained long rows of cheeses, well ripened. Butter was salted in firkins. The surplus of course were articles for market, and one or more trips were made each year to Boston, sixty miles off. The foot leather had not ceased to be tanned in the winter season. A carriage house presented an elegant chaise for the regular journey of the elder persons to the Meeting House Hall on Sunday. The younger people could have the wagon or saddles. . . . Patience, thrift, economy and a rather vigorous character had within the compass of a single life converted a wilderness of forest into the abode of comfortable

independence, not the wealth of the millionaire gained by crafty appropriations of the fruits of other men's labors, by gambling and speculation, but the well earned savings of honest industry and self restraining virtue.[5]

Nathaniel Holmes, who owned this farm described by his grandson, was undoubtedly more successful than many of his neighbors, but there were in the state many more like him, men who in their dignified independence managed their own persons and property successfully and in so doing created a general atmosphere of constructive enterprise. There was also, apparently, something more to be got from all this work than the demonstration of the virtues of prudential management.

It still can be seen that all the ceaseless mowings, choppings, hewings, butcherings, and reapings took place in physical surroundings that were always satisfying and often delightful to the eye. There was the intimacy of the recurring intervales, the gracious line of extending hills rolled out against the horizon, the charm of upland meadows in the sun, the looming grandeur of the higher mountains. Andrew McMillan, a farmer for forty years near Conway, went, as he grew older, for a moment every day to a point on his land where he could see Sunset Hill, the Saco meadows, "and to the North the great range." Asked once by his young nephew why he so regularly performed this silent inspection, he replied "because it is as grand and beautiful as when [I] first saw it." [6] It was possible almost anywhere in the state, if one took the time, to receive such impulses from a vernal wood and, insofar as one can count these things, a good many men like Andrew McMillan did take the necessary time.

One can at least guess as much by the care he and his fellows took to make the forms they created with their own hands fit with the forms imposed by the larger surroundings. The houses, barns, and bridges were settled naturally into the landscape. The row of maples bordering the road in front of the house, the elms flanking the entryway, the lilacs and the rose bush in the

5. George Abbot Morison, *History of Peterborough, New Hampshire*, 2 vols. (Rindge, N.H.: Richard R. Smith, Publisher, Inc., 1954), 1:328–329.

6. Henry McFarland, *Sixty Years in Concord and Elsewhere* (Concord, N.H.: Privately printed, the Rimford Press, 1899), p. 105.

dooryard expressed the civilizing intention that could be achieved by the careful ordering of natural things. The structures—those houses and barns—in their scale, proportion, and masterful organization of interior space were, and still are, elegant models for those seeking the combining principle for use and beauty. And what was put into those old farmhouses, the needed articles for daily life—the ladder-back chairs, the four-posters, the iron crane, the copper kettles, the trestle tables, the corner cupboards, the stencilled walls, the flaxen bedcovers—have passed all tests of time, taste, and feverish acquisition.

So if the investment of beauty in the things one works with every day is a part of truth, then from these instruments and utensils one can deduce that there was, in the private lives of these men and women, a search for saving graces.

What of their more public selves as social beings, members of the town? The town was the fundamental element in the social and political structure of the State. It is hard—probably impossible now—to work down through all the layers of varying definition and interpretation that lie between us and this fundamental element (*Peyton Place, Desire Under the Elms, Ethan Frome, Our Town*, memories of summer vacations, real-estate brochures, calendar pictures in four colors, the genealogical line that leads back through some remote ancestor to a dignifying heritage) to get some feeling for what a New England town really was.

To begin at the unpleasant end of things, there is, of course, a certain amount of truth in the reports of the disillusioned. One of the products of the small, intimate, well-organized community is the sharp tongue and the pharisaical spirit. In each place, there were, beyond doubt, as in Stratham, one or two—or twenty—"ever ready to serve up the character of some good old deacon." [7] And there were those who, in their deviations from the norms, supplied the tongues and spirits with interesting materials. From time to time, as the vital statistics in the town reports suggest, natural desires were irregularly fulfilled under the elms and in the haymows. And then there were the

7. Diary of David Joseph Clark, Dartmouth College Manuscript Collections, Hanover, N.H.

backsliders—those shiftless souls who fell from the grip of the existing orthodoxy. Warren Evans had parishes in Concord, Newport, Lisbon, Candia, and Claremont, and in every place was driven to a rather peevish despair by those who slid away from his ministrations. And then there were those who drank. This, in one way, seemed to include almost everybody. An English traveller was distressed to discover that rum and cider were used, like tea, as a beverage. Jacob Upton of Sharon "carried a wide swathe [in the hayfield] that few could equal." When the drink came round, he would pour out a tumbler level full of New England rum and take it down at one draught, with a tumbler or two of water on top, and the same wide swathe would go forward again as "if his scythe were driven by steam power." [8] Others—a good many others—did not have as steady heads as Jacob Upton. Drinking was indeed a problem. Comments on intemperance appear often in old letters, the temperate objecting forthrightly to the raucous singing and general noisy merrymaking of their inebriate neighbors and pondering the advisability of putting up new dooryard fences to keep out stray animals—and drunks.

Of more violent departures from the norm—crimes such as arson, rape, large-scale theft, murder—there was not much. And the mean-spirited censures, the backslidings, the excursions beyond the bonds of wedlock, the heavy drinking were obviously not often the product of criminal intent or of some generalized depravity. They seem the venting of energies that could not find expression in the ordinary routine, a searching for some further drama in life. On the face of it, what went on in a township was not dramatic. As one sophisticate, David Clark, confided in his diary, here "today's report is yesterday's. The stream that flows over a smooth and even bed presents a smooth, and even, placid surface. Thus, it is with this moral, upright and unenterprising town." [9]

To Franklin Pierce, his birthplace, Hillsborough, seemed tame and monotonous. David Clark was not much of a hand

8. Morison, *Peterborough*, 1:330.
9. Diary of David Joseph Clark.

with a scythe or an axe and believed himself given to change. Franklin Pierce, son of a revolutionary hero and governor, graduate of Bowdoin and friend of Hawthorne, was by birth and experience pulled by or driven toward larger forces. They left their towns, but even those who stayed validated their testimony. Life went on pretty much as usual in Peterborough, Hillsborough, Stratham, Conway, Croydon, Alstead, Orford, Ossipee, Cornish Flat, Winslow's Location, Effingham—in all these towns, today's report was, no doubt, much like yesterday's.

Other men, and good ones, felt the way David Clark and Franklin Pierce did. Daniel Webster, Lewis Cass, Salmon P. Chase, Nathan Appleton, and Horace Greeley followed their courses out of these towns to scenes of larger opportunity. And many more, not so well known, followed them, in considerable number—to Boston, New York or the opening west. Some did not like the farm work on which the whole society was based, some did not like to run the sawmills, grist mills, and small stores that served the agrarian economy; some heard different drummers; and some had other axes to grind. For them, there was insufficient chance to fulfill themselves in the unchanging situation, the course of things as usual. But more stayed put; and of these, most seemed to find an adequate release for normal energy and the satisfaction of enough worldly desires in the work and life of the town.

For one thing, there was, within the settled framework, a great deal going on. If the society was not yet geared up to supply much fabricated distraction—moving pictures, television, snowmobiles—there was much imaginative extension, simplification, and jollification of the day's labor. Those famous huskings, quiltings, bees, and raisings were sensible mixtures of fun and games and hard work. The county fairs were exciting celebrations and dramatizations of what men and women had been doing all year long. Whose apples were reddest, whose oxen moved the stone boat farthest, whose strawberry jam was sweetest, whose horses ran the fastest? The annual encampments of militia produced scenes Breughel would have loved—bright colors, exciting movement, the sense of higher duties to be performed, the sound of music. These were tremendous events attracting all ages, sexes, and conditions for miles around. And it did not matter much if, as the years passed, the urgent sense of combat readiness was displaced by the spirit of carnival. There were also simple pleasures in the timeless mode. Dances were held often. Some communities supported dancing schools or singing schools, and cotillion parties and ceremonial balls were arranged, all well attended. To offset the rigors of winter, parties and tea parties were organized, and sometimes more than a hundred people gathered for sleigh rides.

Beyond these rounds of simple pleasure there were also a series of improving exercises. Foremost among these, perhaps, were those provided by the religious institutions. On the whole, people went on Sunday to the church and, increasingly as the years passed, to different churches. In the year 1819, the state— in the Toleration Act—legally dissolved the historical connection that had previously existed between religion and civil government. The groundwork for the famous law had been laid in 1816 when the strong-willed, idiosyncratic Governor Plumer, a friend of Jefferson, had persuaded the legislature to grant acts of incorporation to any religious association that requested them. The correctness of their tenets, he had said, was a subject that lay between God and conscience, and was one no human tribunal had the right to decide.

Such views and such legislation reflected not only the growing diversity of religious belief but accelerated further division in the ranks of the dominant Congregational faith. Baptists, Methodists, Unitarians, Universalists, and Episcopalians increased steadily in the years before the Civil War. Under such conditions, it appears that the intensity of the ancient faith was somewhat diminished. One ironic observer of the latter-day communicants found them "remarkable for their power to discriminate and appreciate the nice distinctions in the articles of faith they profess to believe." [10] The earlier devotion to a sternly prescribed set of beliefs, never as marked in New Hamp-

10. Diary of David Joseph Clark.

shire as in its neighbors to the south, was, in these times, gradually transmuted—whatever the forms of worship adopted—into what may be thought of as a state of mind. That state of mind was a stoic acceptance, as men struggled to give order to their lives, of those things done by acts of nature and the hand of God—the failure of the crop one year, the burned-down barn another year, the galloping consumption that filled the family lot in the burying ground in any year. But this growing secularization of religious fervor did not profoundly alter the habit of churchgoing. Like Nathaniel Holmes, most men hitched the mare to the chaise and drove their wives to the Meeting House, the children and other relatives riding along behind or following after on foot. In the church, they participated in the rather spare ceremonies and listened to the rather long sermons. Afterwards, in the churchyard, they exchanged the news of the week with neighbors and conducted minor transactions in the exchange of cordwood, hay, or neat stock. Whatever else—by way of expiation of sin and search for salvation—church-going may have meant to particular communicants, it was one of those agreed-upon forms, observed in common, that held the community together.

Considerable segments of the community attended other kinds of improving exercises. These were the exhibitions, debating societies, and lyceums. At stated intervals, people met together to consider whatever topics came into their heads: "The Best Methods of Managing Manure Carried Into the Field in the Fall;" "History of the Cotton Industry in Great Britain: Is the Introduction of Machinery for the Purpose of Abridging Manual Labor Calculated to Promote the Happiness or the Welfare of the Country;" "The Best Method of Disposing of Small Children sent to Winter Schools." Many of these instructive sessions were carefully planned ahead of time.

Less formal and more frequent discussion supplemented such vigorous investigations. What General James Wilson, U.S. congressman and surveyor general of public lands, remembered from his days as a boy in Peterborough many other men could doubtless recall from their youth in other towns.

Many are the noble resolutions that young minds have formed under the shade of the old beech tree. Under that old beech tree, in my young days, the great and talented men of this town used to assemble and to discuss with distinguished power and ability the most important topics. Religion, politics, literature, agriculture, and various other important subjects were there discussed. Well, distinctly well, do I remember those debates. . . . No absurd proposition or ridiculous idea escaped exposure for a single moment. A debater there had to draw himself up close, be nice in his logic and correct in his language to command respectful attention. Abler discussion was never listened to anywhere.[11]

These ceaseless intellectual exercises, formal and informal, served to fortify a public education system that did not work very well. There was not in that society money, time, or manpower to do more than give children the tools for further learning—those celebrated R's. And this, under existing conditions, was hard enough. Within the system, school kept, at odd times and for irregular durations, for a total of about four months a year. Most pupils had no sense that they might venture into further learning beyond the rules of grammar and ciphering. The teachers were young—girls awaiting marriage, boys looking for money (eighteen to twenty dollars) between college terms—or they were old, casehardened restorers of order among the unruly. One of these older men, after a lifetime in the system, called the schools "cattle pens." Another—of whom it was said he could neither read, write, nor cipher—kept what was called the best classes in the district because he could make the boys mind.

One of the most puzzling things in that most puzzling of all processes—learning—is that if such means of instruction did no great good they also did no great—if any—harm. At the least those school houses, no better or worse than most others in the Union, were symbols of the fact that a society struggling to survive by the hardest physical labor set store by the life of the mind. That fact got through to a considerable number of students, who sat dripping with sweat if their place was next to the potbellied stove, frozen stiff if they sat in the back of the room.

11. Morison, *Peterborough*, 1:154–155.

That fact was further established by the existence of those private agencies for learning, such as Exeter and Dartmouth, where a good many young men went on to pursue an education. And the faith in the life of the mind was yet more clearly stated in those lyceums, exhibitions, and conversations under the old beech that older people conducted everywhere. That in combination, all these agencies created a powerful effect in the state can be demonstrated by one of the few pieces of quantifiable evidence available in such matters. In 1850, New Hampshire was one of two states in the Union with an illiteracy rate of less than 2 percent.

10

Managing Affairs

$\mathcal{T}$HE town was not only the center of social and intellectual activity, it was also the agency within which men practiced the art, indispensable in the Jeffersonian scheme, of managing their own affairs. Politics in New Hampshire, worked in the society all year long as an "intermittent fever." The great prescribed occasions were the town meetings in March and the sitting of the legislature in June. But in between times, there were conventions without number to select delegates, nominate candidates, hew out new planks for platforms, and to put party matters in better order. As one observer said, there was never any trouble in getting 100 farmers to a town caucus on any political question, or to attract 1,000 citizens to any state convention. By 1830 any free male adult in the state could vote, and 75 percent of the electorate usually did. In 1837, 87 percent of those eligible cast ballots.

Exercise of the right of suffrage was not the only way citizens participated in the political process. One article of the Jeffersonian faith—that those qualified to vote were also, ordinarily, qualified to hold public office—encouraged many to seek their own advancement; another article of that faith, that there should be frequent rotation in office, gave the opportunity for many to fulfill their ambitions. The result was that a considerable fraction of the population took part in the management of affairs, in what Sam Rayburn (for many years Speaker of the U.S. House of Representatives) later called the foundation of all self-government—the wise exercise of power within one's own ward. For many this meant no more than service in the local offices of the township. Others, starting from these positions, moved onward and upward in the service of the state. William Plumer began as a justice of the peace and selectman in Epping and became, in time, a member of the legislature, speaker of the House, a state senator, a delegate to the state constitutional convention, a member of the United States Senate and governor of New Hampshire. Not everyone—indeed not many—reached such high offices or exerted such a profound influence upon events as this remarkable man, but many who rendered valuable service to the state passed through similar apprenticeships. Benning Bean of Moultonboro was successively justice of the peace, selectman, speaker of the house, president of the senate, member of the governor's council and United States congressman. Men possessed of such experience acquired, through the years, not only understanding of the needs of their society but skill in operating the machinery designed to fulfill those needs.

It was not always necessary to reach the highest offices to exert great influence. The structure of the parties was such that a man of character could become a force in Concord by action from a considerable distance—as did John Taylor Gilman in Exeter and John Wingate Weeks in Lancaster. The great example is Ruel Durkee of Croydon, who carried the state's electoral vote for Lincoln to Washington in 1864 and who served as the model for the hero of American author Winston Churchill's novel, *Coniston*. In the course of his long career, he sat for only two years in the legislature, but for thirty-three years he was selectman and for twenty-eight years town treasurer of Croydon. From this secure base, as Senator Chandler said:

> This stalwart son of New Hampshire who, with little education, no
> early advantages, and living in a poor, rugged, remote country
> town, has made himself a man of great merit, note and power,
> among his fellow citizens and throughout the state. . . . At no im-
> portant crisis in the history of the party, has he failed to be present:

rendering his advice and assistance; always cool, sensible, true and brave.[1]

Although the management of the society was obviously a serious business in which as many citizens as possible were expected to take an active part, politics itself was not regarded as a solemn act. Just as the business of making a living was extended into works of entertainment and celebration, so the political process was often turned into occasions for sociability, jollification, and intense excitement. In Concord, for instance, the party structure served as a way to select members for informal men's clubs. At the Old Phoenix Hotel, the Whigs gathered on almost any cool evening to sit around the fireplace and eat cheese and fruit. There, beneath a grand painting of *Susannah and the Elders*, they talked over the principal issues of the moment and exchanged the local news. The Democrats held similar sessions at the American House.

In the smaller towns, further away from the center of things, the week-long town meetings became a sort of extended holiday. Peddlers arrived with notions, hucksters opened booths on the village green. In the churchyards one could buy cakes, gingerbread, and molasses. Citizens would come into town, spend the day arguing and voting, and return home smelling of rum in their garments.

The great occasion of each year in Concord was inauguration day in June, when the new governor took office and the legislature began its three-week session. For weeks the citizens prepared for this momentous time. Lawns were raked, grounds cleaned up, brass polished, store windows washed. The women bought new dresses and new bonnets. Contracts for the painting of houses contained a clause ensuring that the job would be done by the dawn of the great day. The principal event was an extended military parade before the governor addressed the legislature in the state house. Troops of mounted militia wound through the streets and clattered past an imposing reviewing stand. Beyond the usual stimulation provided by military pag-

1. William E. Chandler, *"Jethro Bass" Unreal* (Concord, N.H.: The Rumford Press, 1906), p. 16.

eantry, there was always the excitement raised by the question
of whether the horses would get out of hand at the command to
draw sabers. They usually did.

The energy expended in political celebration was also in-
vested in the sterner reaches of political life. Argument in town
meetings was invariably long, frequently loud, and often
heated. The caucus, designed to reconcile differences within a
party, was sometimes the agency of explosive conflict. In 1842,
an exhilarating scrimmage between two divisions of Democrats
produced smashed desks, flying wigs, bloody noses on respectable faces, and the pounding of flying feet as they chased each
other up Center Street in Concord. Such turmoil was not taken
as an extraordinary departure from the political norms; it was
understood that on important matters men felt strongly, and that
the way toward ultimate acceptable compromise must, inevitably, be strenuously pursued. As with compromise, so with
votes; the pursuit was strenuous. One town meeting was much
like another. As David Clark suggested in his diary, not a man
that was able to move was ever absent. And from time to time
novel ways were discovered to increase the suffrage. For instance Deacon Caleb Parker, astride a crossbeam in the town
hall of Concord, looked down to see Cyrus Barton, leading citizen, cast his ballot in a close election—twice.

What Governor Plumer said of one unseemly episode in the
Senate—that it was "rude and indecorous"—could also be said,
on the basis of considerable evidence, of the ordinary workings
of the political process in New Hampshire at this time. But, as
often happens when there is a want of decorum, there seems to
have been, on the basis of much available evidence, a great deal
of energy expended in making the process work. The citizens of
New Hampshire seem to have entered into the business of self-
government in the same spirit they brought to the conduct of
their other affairs. Whether they were clearing a field; raising a
house frame; debating at the lyceum the question of whether
machinery increased the sum of human happiness; arranging a
teaparty for twenty-four at Francestown; arguing the merits of
an article in the town warrant; or manipulating the passage of a
bill in the legislature they gave a lot of themselves to the en-

terprise in hand. It was a society fully engaged in furnishing its own support and managing its own affairs. The members were primarily engaged in taking care of themselves—in the process of living rather than in particular products or in the pursuit of some special end. Those who came down with "Boston fever," or wished to make some larger fortune, or sought another music—different drum beats, unheard melodies—found such commitments beyond all doubt "tame," "monotonous," "unenterprising."

The meaning of life for those who remained to work within such commitments is at so distant a remove as today, impossible to assess. One may discover some of it, perhaps, in the thoughts of William P. Tilden. He was a minister who had worn himself out in the effort "to brace up the courage" of a large congregation so that it could confront the great issues of the day—slavery and war. He then went to the small town of Walpole on the Connecticut River. There, in "this pure atmosphere" amid landscapes "both beautiful and delightful," he spent seven very happy years. At home among his "interested worshippers" he felt no call to question their stand on matters of great pith and moment. They were, he said, "a kind and social people" looking for ways to live happily together. His ministry, as he said, was in the service of those trying to understand the meaning of their own personal experience and seeking a fuller awareness of their individual being.[2] That no doubt, was putting a matter which others found tame or monotonous in its very best light but, with due regard for the pressures of charity upon ministerial judgment, it still seems that Mr. Tilden defined, at the least, the aims of many members of this society.

The question remains, how successfully did these members convert their best intentions into working principles, and more particularly, into the terms of public policies? The course of politics in the first half of the last century was disturbed by local differences, conflicts between powerful personalities, confusions in the national political situation, developing change in the

2. William P. Tilden, *Autobiography* (Boston: Houghton Mifflin Company, 1891), pp. 123–124.

way people made their living, and both pressures and attractions exerted upon the state by regions beyond its borders. But, for most of this period, certain persistent attitudes ran through all the complicating circumstances.

Most obvious was the commitment to the Jeffersonian persuasion, expressed first through the Republican party of the founder and later through the Democratic party of Andrew Jackson and his followers. In the beginning, after ratification of the Constitution, the Federalist party had dominated political life. From the southeast corner of the state where the first settlements had been made, the members of this party presided, as the colonial governors had before them, over the affairs of New Hampshire. The power of this region is suggested by the morose judgment of one leading politician that "to run for Governor, a man must remove either to Portsmouth or Exeter, erect or purchase a large, three story house, keep his coach, four horses and servants." [3]

The first indication that the foundations of this Federalist stronghold could be undermined came in 1800. In the election of that year, a principal issue was a bank founded to make small loans on easy terms. In 1799, the Federalist-dominated legislature had closed the institution down. The Jeffersonian Republicans seized upon this act as a blow against the welfare of the common people by the party of money, monopoly, aristocracy, and four-horse coaches. They put up a man for governor who lived in Concord and cut the size of the Federalist majority by almost a third. The source of that majority lay, as it always had, along the seacoast, in the richer river valleys, and in the substantial towns around Monadnock in the southern part of the state. The votes for the Republicans came from the communities in the middle of the state and to the north, and also from the considerable congregation of artisans in the shipbuilding area around Portsmouth. The issues, the voting patterns, and the rhetoric in this election of 1800 were portents of things to come for half a century.

3. David B. Cole, *Jacksonian Democracy in New Hampshire* (Cambridge, Mass.: Harvard University Press, 1970), p. 49.

It took some time, some special events, and the hard work of some remarkable men before the promises of that year were fully redeemed in political power. But by 1822, it could be said that the state was "more decidedly" [Jeffersonian] Republican than any other state in the Union. And shortly after 1829, the year Andrew Jackson took office as president, an organization with a new name, the Democratic party, came into full control of the state, and so remained (with momentary deviations) for years to come.

In all those years, the party—with impressive consistency—stood against those with privilege, aristocratic pretensions, too much money, and monopoly interests. It stood up for what a New York paper called "a low crowd" which meant artisans, laborers, small holders, husbandmen—what were then called, as a hundred years later, the common men. And since in New Hampshire, for most of that time, the majority made their living off the land, a common man was usually a farmer. To him the words of Jefferson in praise of husbandry (suitably translated to meet the needs of journalism and political oratory) were continually directed: the acres of his own, the honest toil, the self respect, the naturalness of his life, the decency, the self-supported independence.

Upon such philosophic foundations the Democratic party leaders built a superstructure of propositions designed to make a more immediate appeal to the hearts and prejudices of their constituency. They put themselves forward as the protectors of the spirit of 1776, the guardians of revolutionary glories. They advocated rotation in office so that all—or at least as many as possible—could have prizes. They saw to it that those who in fact did get the prizes would not profit so much they would join the ranks of privilege. Much was made of the fact, for instance, that a judge made no more than an enlisted man in the navy. And they spoke long and frequently and most favorably of the "plain people of the North," and in all those other directions where plain people tended to vote for them. And they did see to it—as responsible party leaders do—that, as the party acquired power in the federal government, deserving party members were appointed in impressive number to customs houses and post offices around the state. They well knew that the memory of ancient glory and the faiths that moved plain people were no stronger than the power of the political machinery.

Down through the years, that machinery worked very well in the interests of the citizens. The state was one of the first to provide adequate care for the insane. Early on, in 1819, the ancient connection between church and state was severed, a task made easier for Democrats by the fact that the principal churches were Congregationalist and the majority of their communicants were Federalists. At about the same time, imprisonment for debt was prohibited, in an interesting demonstration of how considerations of principle and personal advantage sometimes get mixed up in political action. The law of 1818 established a floor of $13.34—only a man who owed more than this could be sent to jail. This was the exact amount of the indebtedness of Captain Mason Bresser, an old revolutionary hero. The governor signed the bill with annoyed remarks about its particularity, and only because it was a point gained in favor of personal liberty. In the next legislative session, after he had marshalled arguments more general and philosophical, debtors prison was, in effect, abolished for all time. The population in New Hampshire jails was half that of Vermont and a third that of Connecticut in the ensuing two decades. The state's penitentiary system became a model of management and progress in the United States. Throughout these years, repeated efforts were also made to abolish the death penalty.

The state strove in other ways to improve the life of ordinary citizens. While opposing federal aid for internal improvements, state funds were continuously approved for the construction of the roads, bridges, and canals that were so obviously needed by the expanding agrarian economy. And when textile mills began to rise on the landscape, the legislature passed one of the first child labor laws and, somewhat later, limited the number of hours anyone could work in a factory.

Legislation of this sort reflected the essential mood of the state in these years, a mood of thoughtful, constructive, enlightened—if cautious—reform designed to serve the general welfare and to regulate a gradually changing condition. It was also designed to reduce the influence of what Levi Woodbury, a political leader during this period, once called the talented, wealthy, and cunning—by which he meant those who were, in the first instance, Federalists, and later Whigs.

It is hardly surprising that out of a half century of intense engagement in the political process should have come some unusual men, who made a difference not only in New Hampshire but in the nation. The most obvious is one who spent most of his public career in the service of another state and almost all his life in what the majority of New Hampshire men at the time thought of as the wrong party. Yet, in spite of this, Daniel Webster remains the most noteworthy; no history can fail to indicate that, in those years—from across the border and outside the state's dominant political machinery—Webster remained a presence, exerting the power of a myth upon the life of New Hampshire. What he represented to those in the land of his birthplace is best described by the effect he had on even his greatest political enemies. One of them was Isaac Hill, who had fought him for thirty years in New Hampshire and in Washington, with all the considerable weapons at his disposal. The winter before Webster died, Hill told a small boy in a Concord bookstore that he had just seen Webster and that they had talked of farming. Then, almost to himself, Hill added: "And Daniel Webster is the greatest man who ever lived in America." [4]

Certain men, cast in more conventional molds, nevertheless achieved imposing influence in their time. William Plumer, Levi Woodbury, Isaac Hill, Franklin Pierce, and John P. Hale created and maintained a party machinery in New Hampshire that was the envy of politicians in every other state. And by their local successes they were advanced to positions of power in the nation. Hill—a distressed spirit, a tribune of the people, a Jacksonian before Andrew—with an immensely shrewd perception of what the issues were and where the votes lay, was a forceful agent in the Jackson administration. More sophisticated, better trained, though still by Whig standards not sufficiently *suaviter in modo,* was Levi Woodbury. Born in Fran-

---

4. McFarland, *Sixty Years in Concord,* p. 113.

cestown, he had moved to the practice of law in Portsmouth and thus in his own person combined—and carefully exhibited— both the rustic virtues of the countryside and the worldliness of the seacoast. Woodbury was a member of the best senatorial mess in Washington; he and his very attractive wife were leaders in such society as the Jacksonian prejudices established; he spoke during his time in the Senate more than any other member save Hayne and Benton. Though a cautious man, and thus often at odds with Hill, he was a very hard worker and a fair-minded analyzer of events. As senator, secretary of the treasury and associate justice of the Supreme Court, he was a useful public servant for thirty years. Had he not died before the convention, it is probable that he would have been nominated by the Democrats for the presidency in 1852. As things turned out, Franklin Pierce was given that honor.

Pierce was the son of an engaging man who has been called a "noisy, foul-mouthed, hard drinking tavern keeper [who] had chased the red coats out of Concord . . . and suffered with Washington at Valley Forge." [5] Attracted by the revolutionary credentials, Isaac Hill had put the father forward in 1822, as governor, to pull together the votes of common men and sturdy yeomen. The son was an attractive man, a rousing speaker on village greens, and a very successful lawyer before judges as well as juries. Within the state, he proved also to be a shrewd politician, a decisive and, when necessary, ruthless party organizer. In 1852, when he ran for the presidency against Winfield Scott, he carried all but four states. In that same year, John P. Hale was also seeking the presidency as the candidate of the Free Soilers. He had for a long time been one of the leaders of the Democratic party in New Hampshire. Brilliant, lazy, volatile, independent, Hale had worked and fought with Pierce within the party until 1845. In that year, he became an insurgent, with a following of Whigs and Independent Democrats. One year later, he was elected to the United States Senate.

The year 1852 might well be taken as the culminating proof of the power that lay in the Jeffersonian scheme. Common men

5. Cole, *Democracy,* p. 59.

had created and maintained a party that had worked to improve conditions in the state for half a century. They had managed their own affairs with energy, skill, and imagination anchored in good sense. In so doing they had achieved more than a provincial success. From their ranks, experienced men had moved out and up to extend the influence of their faith throughout the nation. Two of these men in 1852 stood for the highest office in the land, and one of them was elected president of the United States.

11

The State and
the Other World

WHAT some men took to be the sun at noon was, in 1852, more realistically an afterglow. The new president was less a symbol of the power of his home state and party than a symptom of the national confusion. And the power of the Jeffersonian scheme in the life of New Hampshire was a fading illusion sustained less by circumstance than by political rhetoric. Events had overtaken the natural course of things. Two great external forces, each beyond local control, had begun to act against the best intentions of the state.

The first great force was the fact of slavery in the South. Slavery had once been a fact in New Hampshire. As early as 1645, a ship commanded by a Captain Smith had brought from Guinea a man who was sold to a Mr. Williams in Portsmouth. In later years sea captains from that port increasingly engaged in the profitable triangular trade. One leg of that triangle ran out to Africa where the ships took on cargoes of black men and women. Most of these people were disposed of, by the conditions of the trade, in the West Indies, but some were brought into New Hampshire for the convenience of the sea captains and their friends. Since black slave labor did not fit easily into the economy of subsistence farming, most slaves could be found in the high-toned quarters around Portsmouth.

Social conditions and the economic organization of New Hampshire, however, did not provide likely ground for the development of slavery, and from the very beginning, many people did not feel very comfortable with the slave trade. Mr. Williams, for instance, had been ordered by the General Court to return the slave he had purchased in 1645 to Guinea. And in all the succeeding years there were men like Jeremy Belknap who, in speaking out against human bondage, spoke for many of their fellows. Some of those who owned slaves undoubtedly did what they could to mitigate and qualify the conditions of slavery which, as a form of human relationship, was not of course subject to mitigation and qualification. Daniel Fowle, a printer, owned a man named Primus who worked beside him in the print shop as a pressman until his death at ninety years of age. General William Whipple—sometime sea captain in the triangular trade, later a Portsmouth merchant, still later a member of the Continental Congress and signer of the Declaration of Independence—owned a man named Prince. As they were setting out together to join the troops that fought against General Burgoyne, General Whipple said to Prince, "from this time on you are your own man." [1]

It was, in fact, the Revolution that put this disturbing institution "in the ultimate course of extinction" in New Hampshire. Those who fought to be free were ready, on the whole, to extend freedom to others. In 1790, there were 158 slaves in the state; a decade later, there were only 8. In 1820, when there were "786 free persons of color in this state," it was said that "the footstep of the slave does not pollute our soil." [2]

At almost the very moment that the state had thus rid itself of the fact of slavery, it was forced into a consideration of the merits of slavery in the abstract. In 1819, when a bill to admit Missouri to the Union came before the House of Representatives in Washington, an amendment was proposed that would prohibit the further introduction of slaves into the new state. By this amendment the great issue that lay between the North and the

1. Adams, *Annals of Portsmouth*, p. 283.
2. Farmer and Moore, *Gazetteer of the State*, p. 23.

NEW HAMPSHIRE

A photographer's essay by Ted Polumbaum

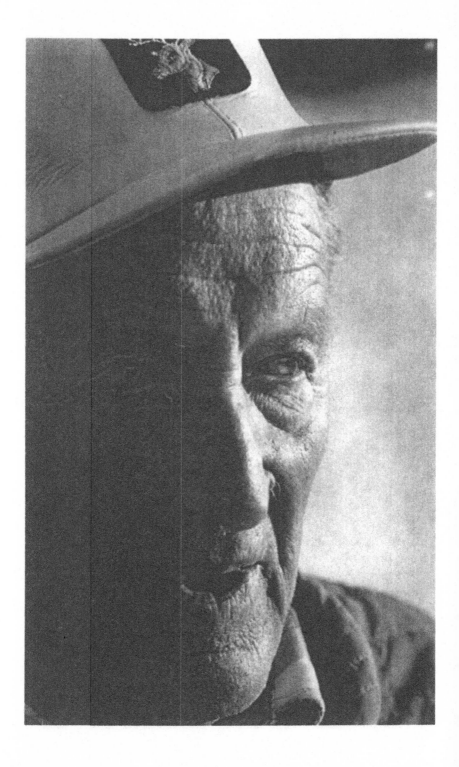

Photos in Sequence

Log lifter at waterpowered sawmill in Fitzwilliam.
Exeter's brass band.
Gathering at Exeter town hall for a band concert.
Eighteenth-century homes at New Castle.
Interior of a house at Shaker Village, Canterbury.
Boat-building shop at Strawbery Banke, a colonial maritime community
  being preserved in Portsmouth.
Restored house built over a stream near Stoddard.
Farmlands at the foothills of the White Mountains.
Cathedral Rock in the White Mountains.
A home with the American flag, Exeter.
Horse-pull at the Newfields Country Fair.
Firemen's "water polo" at the traditional Firemen's Muster, Milford.
Face of a New Hampshire hunter and woodsman.
World Championship sled-dog races, Pittsfield.
Climbers on the Presidential Range on the way to Mt. Washington.

South in this country, almost obscured by skilled maneuver for thirty years, was laid open for all to see. There were months of bitter debate in Congress before the issue was once again resolved, temporarily, by skillful maneuver. But the meaning of the debate had been made obvious.

The legislature of New Hampshire, responding to the discussion in Washington resolved that:

> Slavery is prohibited by the immutable laws of nature, which is obligatory as well on states as individuals. The establishing or permitting slavery by a state, being thus morally wrong, the right to do it, instead of being essential to its sovereignty, cannot exist except only in cases where slavery having already been introduced cannot suddenly be abolished, without great danger to the community." [3]

Continuing, the legislature held that in the given circumstances it could be taken as "a painful necessity" to tolerate "for a time the wrong where the wrong already existed while nothing could justify its extension to new states." [4]

From that time forward the subject of slavery—with its terrible collisions of the practical, prudential, political, and moral—was stuck firmly in the consciousness of men and women in New Hampshire. It was discussed with increasing frequency and intensity in all those lyceums, exhibitions, and Sunday meetings beneath the elms. That many of these discussions, in the 1820s and early 1830s, were conducted in neutral atmospheres appropriate for the objective canvass of a distant situation was probably a fair reflection of the moderate mood of the state in the early days. But the mood, as time passed, was altered by pressures applied both from without and within. Eloquent and determined men from over the borders, who had made up their minds about the wickedness of slavery, saw to it that their views obtained a hearing in New Hampshire. What William Lloyd Garrison had to say in *The Liberator* began to reach a growing audience in the 1830s; his New England Anti-Slavery Society established an outpost in Concord in 1834 and he himself came

---

3. Squires, *The Granite State*, 1:209.
4. Squires, *The Granite State*, 1:209.

often after 1831 to speak in the state. In 1835, John Greenleaf Whittier brought George Thompson, the English lecturer, into the state to speak against slavery. Such influences gave useful support to those in New Hampshire who were seeking to advance the antislavery cause.

Shortly after Whittier's visit, George Stone began to argue the case for abolition and was soon joined by such others as Nathaniel Peabody Rogers and Stephen S. Foster, a young man who left the ministry to devote his energy to the elimination of slavery. Foster often appeared in churches during services to bear testimony against slavery. A brave, passionate, obsessive, exciting man, he was not prepared to retreat one inch from his purpose and made a powerful impression upon the consciousness and conscience of the state.

Men like this, over time, altered the neutral atmosphere and moved the community toward more strongly held positions. Their work was increasingly marked by the kind of perturbing incident that occurs when men feel strongly. Whittier and George Thompson, for instance, were disgracefully mobbed when they came into the state, and Stephen Foster was manhandled out of at least one church in which he was giving impromptu testimony. By 1840, slavery had become a central issue in the life of the community.

When, for instance, William Tilden received a call to Concord from his Massachusetts parish, he felt it necessary to say that he would come for two Sundays to preach two sermons on "the disturbing topics of the day" so that the members of the Concord congregation would "fully understand what they were doing in giving me a call." On his first Sunday, he spoke of the evils of slavery and the necessity for its ultimate abolition. As he concluded his sermon, he saw Stephen Foster—only recently ejected from a church down the street—and Foster's wife in the congregation. Remarking that as a man who was being looked over, he would do what he would do in his own church, he asked Foster or his wife "to say anything which their hearts prompt." Foster rose only to say that he hoped that in time such sentiments as he had just heard would be heard from all the pulpits in the land. After that, Tilden felt, the parish would come to

its decision with "their eyes open." Within the week he was offered, and accepted, the ministry of the church at a salary of
$700 a year.[5]

Confronted by such a clear choice on the great issue as Mr.
Tilden presented to those parishioners, the people of New
Hampshire ordinarily and in time came down on the side taken
by the congregation in Concord. In the endless discussions at
lyceum meetings, in the halls of public debate, and in the Sunday services—wherever the issue was raised as a matter of
philosophical and moral import—it became obvious as time
passed that people were prepared to change their mood and
make up their minds. But within the political process the matter
was far more complicated. There, a change of heart seemed to
disturb the arrangements men had so earnestly constructed out
of necessary compromise to give improving order to their lives
together. The career of John P. Hale suggests as much.

In 1835, when he was a leader in the Democratic party in the
state and a United States attorney appointed by Andrew Jackson, he went to a meeting called by George Storrs, an abolition-
ist minister. At that meeting, Hale attacked with all his force the
whole notion of abolition and argued that slaves were merely
"beasts in human shape." Ten years later, however, he stood
up at the Old North Church in Concord, pointed a finger at his
old college friend and political comrade-at-arms, Franklin
Pierce, and said—in words now carved on his statue in the park
in front of the State House—

> I may be permitted to say that the measure of my ambition will be
> full, if when my early career shall be finished and my bones be laid
> beneath the soil of New Hampshire, when my wife and children
> shall repair to my grave to drop the tear of affection to my memory,
> they may read upon my tombstone, "He who lies beneath surren-
> dered office, place, and power, rather than bow down and worship
> slavery." [6]

As Mr. Hale later explained, he had gradually seen the light
over those ten years, and because for much of that time he had

5. Tilden, *Autobiography*, pp. 107–108.
6. McClintock, *History of New Hampshire*, p. 593.

held public office, his change of mind was attended with great public consequences. In 1842, he had gone to the Congress of the United States as a totally convinced Democrat. He was against the Bank, federally supported internal improvements, imprisonment for debt, and the protective tariff. He was for states rights, economy in government, and the abolition of West Point. But he found on his arrival in Washington that the real issues were the right of petition and the annexation of Texas—in other words, the issue of slavery. Standing Rule 21 of the House required that all petitions to Congress having to do with slavery should be laid on the table (that is, neither debated nor considered). Hale allied himself with John Quincy Adams in his great fight against this gag rule and in 1844 voted, alone in the New Hampshire delegation, for the successful amendment to the House rules that eliminated Rule 21.

On the matter of Texas, in 1844 Hale—with the other members of his delegation—was under instruction from the New Hampshire legislature to support annexation at the earliest possible moment. In January 1845, he presented a set of re-solves to Congress proposing the elimination of slavery from a large section of the state in the event that it should be added to the Union. These resolves were defeated. He then composed a long letter to his constituents telling them he could not be an agent in the annexation of a foreign country for the avowed pur-pose of sustaining and perpetuating human slavery. Such a mea-sure he declared to be "eminently calculated to provoke the scorn of earth and the judgement of heaven." [7]

Confronted by such an act of insubordination, the Democratic state committee, for two decades the controlling agency in the legislature and the ruling authority in the politics of the state, acted with dispatch and decision. A convention to nominate a new man for Hale's seat in Congress met in February. At the bottom of it all was Hale's old friend, Franklin Pierce, who travelled all round the state to rouse party members against their Congressman. It was in the course of this effort to read Hale out

7. *Exeter News-Letter,* January 20, 1845.

of the party that the two men had faced each other at the turbulent meeting in the Old North Church.

Each side had enough support to produce, for a time, a deadlock. But by the end of February, enough members of the party, under the leadership of Amos Tuck of Exeter, had gone into the Hale camp to force decisive action. On February 22, in a special convention, these men who supported the position of their Congressman, established a new party—the Independent Democrats. A tug-of-war followed, in the course of which the seat of John Hale lay empty and the Whigs, taking advantage of the divided opposition, stepped into the governorship in 1846. Confronted by these symptoms of growing disarray, Pierce moved rapidly and effectively to restore some order in his party, but the fact remains that the classic solidarity of the Democrats was never quite the same again.

Some years earlier, old John Wingate Weeks had foreseen such possibilities and had written to Franklin Pierce—in part to warn him of impending trouble and in part to strengthen Pierce's resolve. Weeks was an old and wise man. A veteran of the War of 1812, a very successful farmer, a large landholder in Lancaster—he had been a power economically, socially, and politically in the whole North Country for forty years. In 1839, he said to Pierce:

> I hope never to see the day when slavery, in the horrible forms in which it presents itself in our beloved country, shall be identified with the principles of that party to whom we must look (under God) for all we hold dear in the world. This subject and that of the reserved rights of the states, should not often be touched and then with great delicacy and forebearance. But you are aware of all these [considerations]. Therefore maintain the character you have thus far sustained. . . . Of all the multitudes of Republicans in ancient and modern times, found in the lower walks of life, how few have retained their principles after their elevation to power.[8]

At that time John Weeks laid upon Franklin Pierce an obligation that, as many good Democrats were to find in the days

8. Papers of John W. Weeks, Dartmouth College Manuscript Collections, Hanover, New Hampshire.

ahead (especially New Hampshire Democrats) would be very
hard to keep. For a generation, these men had directed the party
machinery that had made the liberal spirit a leaven in the life of
the state. And for a generation, they had been powers in the national party; they had helped to design the system of alliances
between men of the North and men of the South that had insured the dominance of that party. Much of the authority they
had achieved at home depended on their faithful commitments
to the national party, which had control over the distribution of
the loaves and fishes of politics. So they were bound by many
practical considerations to support the party structure. And there
was also a higher ground. What men held dear in that world
seemed held together by the Union, and the Union would more
probably be preserved, not by the Whigs with their precarious
coalition of special interests and old heroes, or the Free Soilers
with their arbitrary propositions, but by the Democrats whose
writ was designed to run generally East and West and North and
South.

Eventually, as John Weeks had foreseen, there came a time
when, in the interests of that general appeal, slavery got mixed
up with the principles of the party. The leading men in New
Hampshire then discovered that they were the captives of their
own previous success as prominent figures in the national councils of the Democratic party. What had happened to the party
around the country began to happen at home. In the 1840s, as
the great issue pushed itself ever farther into the public consciousness, there was increasing tension along all the party
lines. By the end of the decade, there were disturbing fissures in
the party's structure. In 1848, Lewis Cass, born in Exeter, for a
decade a successful proconsul in the territory of the Middle
West, and a resident of Michigan was nominated by the party
for the presidency. He lost the election to Zachary Taylor because that devoted Democrat, Martin Van Buren, abandoned his
ancient allegiances to run for president on the Free-Soil ticket.
Clearly, the strains imposed by the issue of slavery were
seriously jeopardizing the carefully arranged intersectional
agreements on which the party depended.

Franklin Pierce and his associates acted quickly and with resolution to restore a measure of order within the state party. At the same time, having in mind the national situation they began, as sensible politicians, to "trim their sails to catch the southern breeze." [9] Deploring slavery as a moral and social evil, they nevertheless maintained, as an article of party faith, that the future of slavery could be determined only by the citizens of the states and territories where it existed. External agitation and general party professions on the subject would simply aggravate the problem. This was, in effect, the principle of "squatter sovereignty" later put forward by Stephen A. Douglas.

Such an effort to accommodate the issue saved the day at a time when it was beginning to seem that saving a day in the life of the society was increasingly important. It also turned the eyes of party members in the nation toward New Hampshire. To reclaim the presidency in 1852 required a northern man because most of the votes were in the North, but also a man who had demonstrated some sympathy for the South. Lewis Cass had turned out to be a loser in 1848, and Van Buren had turned his back on his party in the same election. But in New Hampshire there was Levi Woodbury, a justice of the Supreme Court, a man who had served Andrew Jackson, a moderate who believed that the laws supporting slavery must be obeyed until repealed. But, in 1851, Levi Woodbury died and Franklin Pierce— soldier in the Mexican War, friend of Jefferson Davis, United States Senator without much of a record of any kind, skilled and experienced architect of local political situations—was put forward. He, as much as anyone, had determined how his party in New Hampshire would stand on slavery and he had apparently restored party order after the difficulties of the 1840s. In 1852, he was elected president of the United States.

To some contemptuous Whigs, he was a "New Hampshire Democrat, a kind of third rate county, or at most, state politician." [10] To many others he was a northern man with southern principles—a "doughface." In any case, he was not a success. It is not clear that anyone else seeking the same objectives

9. Squires, *The Granite State*, 1:219.
10. Squires, *The Granite State*, 1:219.

would have done much better. His hope, like the hope of the far abler Stephen A. Douglas, was that by political accommodation the party—East, West, North and South—could be held together, and that a party so unified could save the Union. He and those like him did not understand that the divided feelings of the country had gone beyond the reach of compromising effort and adroit accommodation. Even in the home state, John P. Hale, driven out of the Democratic party in 1845, continued to be elected to the Senate by a coalition of Whigs and Independents. And in the same year, Amos Tuck was sent to Congress as an opponent of slavery by this same coalition.

Seven years later, in 1853, fourteen men—Hale and Tuck among them—met in Exeter to start a new political organization which, at the suggestion of Tuck, they called the Republican Party. In 1854, the Democrats lost the governorship to the Know-Nothings (a nationalist and antiforeign party) and in 1856, for the first time in eight presidential elections, the Democrats lost the state to John C. Fremont.

New Hampshire, like any other state in the Union, could not seal itself off from the disruptive forces let loose by the fact of slavery. The further fact that, within the state, there were so many men and women who stood ready to follow in the path of Stephen Foster, William Tilden, Amos Tuck, and John P. Hale simply intensified the conflict of feelings as the society moved steadily away from its previous attitudes and habits of mind. Because what at first seemed to be a political issue was, at bottom, a moral matter for these citizens, the intensifying feelings of the 1850s could no longer be satisfied or contained by the political maneuvers of the skilled, experienced Democratic leadership. The party organization began to disintegrate and, insofar as that organization had given structure to the Jeffersonian scheme of things, that structure also started on a disintegrating course.

A second kind of force was also acting against that scheme of things as the years went by. It had its source in those workshops that Thomas Jefferson had proposed to keep in Europe and out of America. The trail of this accumulating energy ran far back in the history of the state. In 1633 one of the proprietors in England had sent a model of a sawmill to men in the Piscataqua region. From that time on, there was machinery in New Hamshire. Mechanization, designed to support the farmer's way of life, developed slowly but steadily through two centuries. Two of the primary needs were served by water-powered sawmills and gristmills that, along with the Town House, church, school, and burying ground, were the foundations of every community. By 1810, there were 710 sawmills and 611 grist mills in the state. Manufacturing of other kinds grew more slowly. In that same year, there were 236 tanneries, 19 linseed-oil mills, 18 distilleries, 5 iron furnaces, 14 nail factories, and 6 paper mills. The products of all this enterprise were consumed almost wholly within the state. Two impressive exceptions may be made from this list of small local ventures serving local constituencies. Over on the coast, in the shipyards of the district of Portsmouth, about ten vessels a year were built from 1800 to 1850. And, beginning in 1813 in Concord, the firm that became Abbott, Downing and Company began to build the legendary Concord coaches. The ships, of every type, were as good as could be found, and the coaches were the best of their kind. It is not merely pardonable pride that claims that these ships and coaches must, on any list of manufactures, seem exceptional. Both in their making and in the finished results they were less the products of the workshop than works of art.

A good many other towns had, like Portsmouth and Concord, had their own special, if less exceptional, interests. What happened in New Ipswich happened also in many neighboring communities. It was a "post town" which, in the last quarter of the eighteenth century, had a population of about 1,000 people. Most of them made a living off the land, but there were several establishments for making things. One made potash and pearlash, another made earthenware, a third produced linseed oil from the local flax, a fourth manufactured small quantities of glass, and a fifth turned out an oatmeal concoction from a secret formula brought into town by a Scotsman named James Barr. (This was sold to Boston apothecaries.) There was also a small fulling mill by the waterfall. Fulling, a process for shrinking and strengthening cloth as it came loose-woven from a hand loom, was one of the few stages in the making of fabric that could be mechanized in this country in the last quarter of the eighteenth century. Two wooden hammers, fixed to a camshaft driven by a water wheel, delivered alternate blows to cloth as it lay in a fulling solution.

Just as the century turned, a new machine to take the place of men at another stage of making cloth was introduced in New Ipswich. Charles Barrett, a farmer, a land owner, a man of vision, and a shrewd coordinator of local energies invited a man named Charles Robbins to come to town. Robbins had worked in Rhode Island with a man named Samuel Slater, who had spent time as an apprentice in one of those workshops of Europe—a textile mill in England, to be exact. In 1789, Slater had come to this country in what would today be called a covert operation, with the plans for the English mill and machinery in his head. From memory, he had constructed a factory in 1793 for the spinning of cotton in Pawtucket, Rhode Island. Charles Robbins had worked in this factory, and when he came to New Hampshire in 1803, he built from memory a factory in New Ipswich. That is the way industrial information was passed on, in those days. A good many men like Robbins came out of Pawtucket to put what they remembered into the foundations of the textile industry in the small towns of New England. In New Ipswich, Robbins built a mill of 500 spindles. On December 15, 1804, this mill—the first in New Hampshire—made four and a half pounds of yarn.

What had happened in New Ipswich in these years happened in a good many other New Hampshire towns. Enterprising local men got together to launch new ventures that Alexander Hamilton, the great opponent of Thomas Jefferson, had said, in his *Report on Manufactures,* were necessary for the development of the country. In Peterborough, for instance, a mill was incorporated in 1808. The machinery was put together by John Field, who had worked in the Slater Mills in Pawtucket. One hundred shares of stock, each worth $135, were issued. Half the amount was subscribed by men from Amherst; the other half was taken up by twenty Peterborough residents. Almost all were descendants of the original settlers; almost all were farmers. That among them they could raise about $7,000 (a sizable sum at the time) for a new and uncertain venture suggests how successfully they had administered their farms in previous years.

Because there were a good many men like these in other towns, similar in means and spirit, there were by 1820 fifty-one textile mills in the state, about evenly divided between cotton and wool. Most of them were in the southern counties; all of them, of course, were set by the side of a running stream; and almost all were built of red brick, in rectangular form, and in that scheme of proportion and scale that still seems perfect. Most of these factories were financed by local money, employed twenty or twenty-five local people, and served, on the whole, nearby markets. As in their physical presence they fitted eas-ily—and often gracefully—into the natural surroundings, so they fitted easily and appropriately into the life of the communi-ties in which they were built.

About the time things were getting started in Peterborough, a mill was being built in a much smaller town named Derryfield. This one was built by a man named Benjamin Prichard who, as a carpenter, had helped Charles Robbins in the construction of the first mill in New Ipswich. He came to Derryfield with some secondhand machinery taken from one of the Slater factories, obtained some water rights from a man named James Harvey, and put up a little mill for the manufacture of cotton goods. From James Parker and David McQuisten of nearby Bedford, and Samuel Kidder and John Stark, Jr. (the son of the great rev-olutionary hero), Robbins obtained the funds to start his ven-ture. It all started as it had in New Ipswich, Peterborough, Keene, Hillsborough, or Harrisville and there was little reason in the first days to expect that Prichard's mill would be any dif-ferent from the rest—twenty-five men, a small brick building, a whir and clack of mechanism all fitting easily into the natural surroundings.

Derryfield was on the Merrimack River a few miles below Concord. The mill site was beside a falls where, from time im-memorial, Indians had come in the spring to catch alewives, shad, and salmon. They thought of it as a sacred place. Around these falls, at the turn of the century, an extraordinary man named Samuel Blodget had built a canal designed to connect Concord with Boston by water. He had conceived this project at the age of seventy, after a career of imaginative dealing in lumber, land, animals, potash, furs, and fine linens—at a time when no one in this country knew how to build a canal. Fourteen years later, in 1807, he took a small boat through the channel he had constructed and then, almost immediately, he died. Within a few years there was steady trade between Concord and Boston—five days upstream, four days downstream in cargo carriers of the Merrimack Boating Company.

For Samuel Blodget, the idea of a canal had been incidental to a larger scheme. He was one of those who, in the first days of the Republic, had detected imperial possibilities in the surrounding wilderness. Standing once by the construction site at the falls, he had said, "As the United States grows we must have manufactures and here at my canal will be a manufacturing town that shall be the Manchester of America." [11]

The falls around which the canal had been built, and where Benjamin Prichard constructed his little mill, were set in what Jeremy Belknap described as a "delightful landscape of verdant banks, cultivated fields and distant hills." The river at this place dropped "in three large pitches, one below the other" about "eighty feet in the course of a half mile." Racing through the several passages in "majestic" turmoil, the falling water made a roar that could be heard from several miles away. In the solid rock of the riverbed, the pounding water had—over the centuries—reamed out holes "exactly round," eight feet in diameter, and three or four feet deep. The Indians had once used these strange holes to hide their provisions in times of war, and believed that the whole site had been laid out in accordance with some divine and particular plan. This was the Amoskeag fall, and it was one of the great sources of water power in the country at the time. [12]

The mill that was started there with local money was forty feet square, built of brick and, at first, contained eighty-five

11. Maurice D. Clarke, *Manchester* (Manchester, N.H.: J. B. Clarke, 1875), p. 21.
12. Belknap, *History of N.H.*, 3:59–60.

spindles. It grew slowly. About 1812, an Arkwright spring frame was added and then, in 1819, a Cartwright power loom. By 1813, the four original proprietors had become twelve share-holders—all local men and most of them farmers. None of them alone, nor all of them together, had the money to finance further expansion, so they turned to Samuel Slater in 1822. He lent them $5,000 and put them in touch with people in Mas-sachusetts who knew something about the textile business. For the next fifteen years the establishment slowly expanded. Land surrounding the falls was bought up, three new mill buildings were constructed, water-power rights along the banks of the Merrimack were gradually extended. By 1835, the Amoskeag Manufacturing Company held 700 acres of land, had a net worth of $120,000, and was owned by 19 stockholders—still, for the most part, local men. In the following year, 1836, the number of stockholders increased to seventy-three—most of them new people living in Massachusetts. Among them were men named Lyman, Appleton, Lowell, Amory, Lawrence, Pickman, and Warren—great names in the history of Mas-sachusetts, in the field of finance, and in the development of the textile industry.

Nathan Appleton, born in New Ipswich, had gone to Boston at the age of fifteen in 1794. During the next twenty years he had made a good deal of money as a merchant. In 1813, he in-vested $5,000 in the mill Francis C. Lowell was building to make cotton cloth in Waltham, Massachusetts. Lowell, support-ing his memory of what he had seen in the factories of Europe with a mechanical imagination that amounted to genius, in-troduced many improvements in existing mill machinery. Far more significantly, he juxtaposed his various machines in such a way that he created a new kind of mill system "which contained all the operations of converting raw cotton into finished cloth." [13] In 1814, his new works went into operation, and in the next two years he and Nathan Appleton established the es-sential principles on which the textile industry in this country

13. *Dictionary of American Biography*, 20 vols. (New York: Charles Scribner's Sons, 1928–1937), 11:456.

was founded: the concentration of all the powered machines needed to make cloth in one place; cheap—usually female—labor; a separate selling organization to insure the widest possible markets.

Using these principles and supporting them with money from the Boston investors, the men from Waltham first built a textile factory, and then a town around that factory along the banks of the Merrimack River. The factory became famous in the 1820s and 1830s as a marvelous producer of cotton cloth and as a place where some men and more women worked in attractive, enlightened surroundings. The men behind this venture were respecters of mechanical efficiency and money, but as churchmen and citizens of the new world they also respected human beings. Therefore, they sought to build into their new manufacturing system ways to protect the bodies, support the morals, and improve the minds of those who worked within the system. The town they built was called Lowell, in memory of Francis C. Lowell, who died in 1817. When the mills had first been put at the site, there were about twelve houses along the river. Twenty-five years later the population of the city was 32,621, most of whom, one way or another, were connected with the mills.

In 1837, the men who had made Lowell—Nathan Appleton was by that time called the Great Manufacturer in Boston—brought their methods, money, principles, and good intentions to the Amoskeag Manufacturing Company. More land was acquired, more machinery was constructed, more water rights were obtained, more mills were built. On the east side of the river, a model city was laid out with two big town squares, sites for schools, churches, parks, and cemeteries. Six blocks of houses—tenements—were built solidly of brick and wood for the families who worked in the mills. In 1838, fifty people lived within what later became the limits of the city of Manchester. Eight years later there were 10,000 inhabitants—more than in Concord, which had been there for 125 years, more than in Portsmouth, which had been there since the beginning. In 1846, the mills in Manchester consumed 9.6 million pounds of cotton to make 22.5 million yards of cloth—which works out to forty

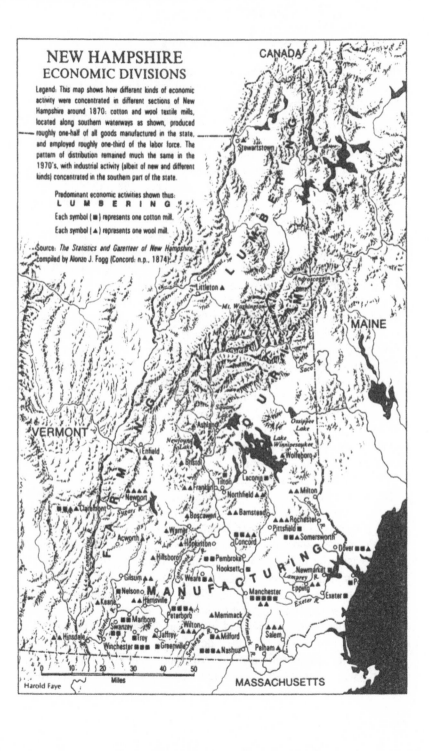

NEW HAMPSHIRE
ECONOMIC DIVISIONS

Legend: This map shows how different kinds of economic
activity were concentrated in different sections of New
Hampshire around 1870: cotton and wool textile mills,
located along southern waterways as shown, produced
roughly one-half of all goods manufactured in the state,
and employed roughly one-third of the labor force. The
pattern of distribution remained much the same in the
1970's, with industrial activity (albeit of new and different
kinds) concentrated in the southern part of the state.

Predominant economic activities shown thus:
L U M B E R I N G

Each symbol (■) represents one cotton mill.

Each symbol (▲) represents one wool mill.

Source: *The Statistics and Gazetteer of New Hampshire,*
compiled by Alonzo J. Fogg (Concord: n.p., 1874).

CANADA

MAINE

VERMONT

MASSACHUSETTS

Harold Faye

0 10 20 30 40 50
Miles

miles of yardgoods a day. To achieve this astounding result, 2,500 females and 700 males—many of whom lived in 109 tenements built by the company—worked from 6:30 in the morning to 7:30 at night, with a 35-minute nooning. What had begun fifty years before as an exercise of local and individual enterprise had become a marvel of systematic organization, production in mass, and world-wide distribution.

In this way, the workshops that had started the industrial revolution in Europe were brought to New Hampshire. At about the same time, a second product of that revolution made its entry into the state. In 1830, a man named James Hayward drew up a plan for a railway to run from Boston through New Hampshire and on to unidentified parts of New York. Nothing came of it. In 1831, there was some talk of a railway from Nashua to Windsor, Vermont. Nothing came of that, either. This was hardly surprising, since the first locomotive in the country had moved on rails in the year 1829—and it had then moved only a few hundred feet. But by the middle of the 1830s, experiments in other states had demonstrated that steam transport was altogether possible. In 1835, the legislature chartered a railroad to run between Nashua and Lowell. It was opened in 1838, and two years later a road beginning in Boston ended at Exeter. By 1840, there were about fifteen miles of railway in the state. It was not much, but it was enough to excite the anxieties of many citizens about the developing future.

The place of the railroads became a matter of public debate. On the one hand, it was argued that the new invention, like the textile mills, was evidence of a new dispensation, a mark of further progress. On the other hand, it was argued that between canals, roads, and turnpikes there was already sufficient transport. Also, the railroads would ruin the horse business, destroy the hay market, kill cows, and break down in winter. Furthermore, in order to build a right-of-way, it was obviously necessary to interfere with the rights of private property.

The debate over the railroad was soon extended to include all the other apparatus in the developing system of industrialism—banks, corporations, credit, and money—which, quite often, was Massachusetts money. The question, "Is the Introduction of Machinery for the Purpose of Abridging Manual Labor Calculated to Promote the Happiness or the Welfare of the Country?'' was frequently asked from the platforms of the lyceums. And from the realm of public discussion, the topic entered into politics and, specifically, into the deliberations of the Democratic party. That party had been the custodian of the way of life defined by its original founders; it had also, for half a century, been the principal source of the energy that supported the concept of gradual social progress. Now it became increasingly clear that there was a developing conflict between the way of life that was held dear and the new kind of progress. Whether the party leaders who assembled in Concord looked down the river to the dramatic changes in Manchester; or pondered how to find more money without sinking into deeper vassalage to the Boston banks; or considered how to move the rising tide of farm and factory goods without dislocating the old ways of landholding they confronted very hard choices. And the need to choose created a division within the party itself.

As time went on into the 1840s, the fundamental issue became shockingly clear: whether the residents of the state wanted to go on living as they had been living, or whether—out of the new materials and energies available—they wished to create a new way of life. There was also bound up in this issue a further question, not then so obvious to people who had long been schooled to manage their own lives: whether the accumulating materials and expanding energies could create conditions of living that would, in time, be beyond the power of men to order and control in their own best interests.

For some time, those who preferred the way things had been, the men who had been the backbone of the party for half a century, maintained the ascendancy. In 1840, they put through the legislature a law accepting the principle that all railroads already chartered could exercise the right of eminent domain to obtain land for their rights-of-way, but could not begin to build until all claims against them had been paid. Furthermore and specifically, future railroads would no longer have the right to acquire land through eminent domain. Two years later, the legislature passed a bill making a stockholder in any corporation personally responsible for the debts and civil liabilities of that corporation. This act eliminated from company charters the principle of limited liability, which had been the foundation of corporate stability. By these two pieces of legislation, the legislature consciously sought to construct a barrier that would protect the high ground of the past against the racing tide of industrial development.

These laws were not enacted without doing great damage to the party machinery. The old leaders, like Hill and Woodbury, and the young men coming on, like Hale and Pierce, found themselves arrayed against each other with varying degrees of intensity. Isaac Hill, for instance, would begin every speech with compelling descriptions of the pastoral democracy that had been developed in the state, but he would then move slowly into a defense of the new dispensation as befitted his status as an adroit politician, a land owner, and a holder of corporate shares. John Hale, on the other hand, was what was then called a radical because he profoundly distrusted all the apparatus of industrial development. Franklin Pierce, the rising power, seemed at first to hold with those who advocated industrial progress, but switched to the other side when he came back from his service in Washington. Hill dourly asserted that this change of heart occurred when a group of farmers retained him as counsel in a suit against the railroads. Levi Woodbury, after his usual scrupulous study of the situation, came out as usual somewhere in the middle. He said in a speech in 1841 that private corporations were good for some purposes, especially if the ends were great and hazardous, but they were ridiculous for most public objectives—like transport.

Such differences of opinion were in the nature of things. These successful men had come out of a past where most important things seemed to stay the same; they had been there and it worked. Now they were seeking, without useful precedent, to prepare themselves and their fellows to deal with what seemed to be an unknown but quite different kind of future. So within the old party, both the leaders and the rank and file were at odds with one another. And when, in the later 1840s, the question of slavery was added to party deliberations, the solid structure—so carefully built up through the decades—slowly came apart under the accumulating pressures. And with the shaking of the structure came the decay of the ancient Jeffersonian scheme.

The divisions in the Democratic party were not, of course, a first cause of the decay of that scheme. It—and the party—were undermined by conditions beyond their control. The issue of slavery was, for New Hampshire as for the rest of the Union, a paralyzing distraction for two decades before the Civil War. The force of industrial development created perhaps a less obvious— but in the long run a more powerful—obstacle to the continuance of politics and life as usual. The conscious effort of the community, as expressed by the acts of the legislature in 1840 and 1842, to neutralize that force proved inadequate before the irresistible march of events.

For a time the effort seemed to succeed. In the five years after 1840, only fifty-six miles of track were laid in the state. From 1840 to 1843, there were no new charters for manufacturing corporations and only nine for other kinds of financial and commercial institutions. But by 1844, the citizens began to discover that what they sought to limit in their own state was in fact marvelously expanding elsewhere. There was a growing fear that the web of rails that was spreading in the surrounding states would leave New Hampshire unsupported and unconnected in the center. Also, the money from Boston began to flow in other directions. Specifically, it was rumored that $1 million that might have gone to the further development of Manchester had been diverted to Maine.

So, swept along by growing opposition to the maintenance of things as they had been, the legislature in the mid-1840s altered the concept of unlimited liability for individual stockholders and returned the right of eminent domain to the railroads. The pent-up energy in the system soon made itself felt. In 1846 and 1847, 123 charters were granted to manufacturing corporations with a combined value of $23 million. Railroad mileage rose from about 20 in 1840 to 375 in 1845. By 1850, New Hampshire had more miles of track than all but one of the surrounding New England states.

Still, those seeking to control the course of industrial development retained enough strength to pass limiting and ameliorating legislation. They created a board of commissioners with the power to lay out railway lines; to investigate each petition from a railroad that sought to exercise the right of eminent domain and recommend an action to the governor; and to reduce rates if profits exceeded 10 percent. In addition, the state was given the power to repossess any road after twenty years, as well as the power to insist that a service once started must be continued. And finally, as an indication that the ancient faith in the independent husbandman had not disappeared, any citizen was given the right to run his own cars on any railroad tracks. By 1852, the legislature had also passed laws restricting child labor, imposing a ten-hour day for factory work, and giving the legislature the right to revoke any charter. Finally, the legislature curtailed the issuance of passes by the railroads and made it illegal to charge more for a short haul than for a long one.

By these actions, New Hampshire put itself in the forefront of those states seeking to introduce some order to the course of industrial development. It also demonstrated a remarkable foresight about the difficulties that would inevitably attend industrial development in the years to come. For such prevision it paid penalties. In the twenty years before the Civil War, capital increased more slowly in New Hampshire than in most neighboring states, and the population grew more slowly than in most of the Union.

For this condition, of course, there were other attendant causes—social, political, economic. In the years to come these causes, intensifying, would more and more give shape to the life of men and women in New Hampshire. Anyone looking forward in the year 1860 would have been hard put to it to anticipate the character and quality of life that would develop in the next fifty years. And anyone looking back over a hundred years could well conclude that, as things go in the history of any society, it had been a great run of time.

12

The War of the Rebellion

*M*ARCH 1, 1860, was a mud-time day in Concord. Wild grey sky, gusting winds, showers of rain flecked with snow, sloppy underfoot, feeling much colder than it really was. At two o'clock in the afternoon, Abraham Lincoln spoke at Phenix Hall. Probably the only man in the state who knew him personally was Amos Tuck, but the big hall was jammed with people. During the hour-long speech, there was the accumulating drama that attended so many Lincolnian performances. First, the puzzled uneasiness before the strange presence on the platform; then the gradual accommodation to abnormalities of manner, dress, and diction; next, a sort of unperceived shift into gathering attention; and finally, total absorption in "one of the most powerful, logical, compacted speeches to which it was ever our fortune to listen." [1]

From Concord, Lincoln went, during the next three days, to Manchester, Dover, and Exeter. At each place, the effect was the same: "We are not extravagant in the remark that a political speech of greater power has rarely, if ever, been uttered." [2]

1. Leon Burr Richardson, *William E. Chandler, Republican* (New York: Dodd, Mead and Company, 1 1940), p. 33.
2. Richardson, *William E. Chandler,* p. 33. The fullest study of this subject is Elsin L. Page's *Abraham Lincoln in New Hampshire* (Boston: Houghton, Mifflin Company, 1929).

What brought Lincoln into the state was a chain of circumstances, mostly personal, that ran a good way back. In 1847, Amos Tuck, like John P. Hale, had left the Democratic party and had been elected to Congress by a combination of Whigs and Independents. During the term Lincoln served as a Congressman, Tuck met him; they agreed on the slavery question, and struck up a friendship. When Tuck left Washington in 1853, he returned to Exeter. There he practiced law and began, with his usual combination of patience and common sense, those negotiations that caused his followers later to claim "that the Republican Party was really a New Hampshire creation." [3] By 1859, Tuck was one of the most powerful men in the state. He was also a trustee of Phillips Exeter Academy.

In that year, Robert Todd Lincoln entered the academy, apparently because Amos Tuck lived in the town. Some months later, word reached Exeter that Abraham Lincoln proposed to visit his son in the early spring. Learning of this plan, Amos Tuck—or perhaps Nehemiah G. Ordway, the chairman of the state Republican committee—asked Lincoln if he would be willing to take some part in the state campaign that was nearing its close. Lincoln accepted the invitation and spent the days from March 1 to March 4 in the state.

The reason Lincoln had come to the East in the first place was that the Young Men's Central Republican Union of New York City had asked him to give the final lecture in a series of talks on political subjects. On February 27, 1860, he appeared at the Cooper Institute before a large assemblage of the "intellect and moral culture of the city." There he gave one of the great speeches of his life. As he ended, "hats and handkerchiefs went into the air." No man, it was said, "on his first appeal had ever before made such an impression on a New York audience." To at least one reporter, he seemed "the greatest man since St. Paul." [4]

From such a dazzling reception in such forbidding terrain, Lincoln proceeded to New Hampshire. His further travels in-

3. *Dictionary of American Biography,* 19:28.
4. Carl Sandburg, *Abraham Lincoln, The Prairie Years,* 2 vols. (New York: Harcourt, Brace and Company, 1926), 2:214.

cluded Rhode Island and Connecticut, where he ended his tour in New Haven with words about the right of free labor to strike that have been quoted ever since. Wherever he went on this trip, there was that same rapt attention followed by wild enthusiasm. When he returned home from "his triumph in New York and New England" he told William Herndon that, for once in his life, he had been "abashed by his personal appearance" and his ill-fitting clothes. He also came home with "his self-confidence stimulated to unwonted proportions." "It was apparent now to Lincoln," said Herndon, "that the Presidential nomination was within his grasp." [5]

There is a theory, held by several men who have written about the history of New Hampshire, that this contingency first became apparent to Lincoln sometime during the four days he spent on New Hampshire ground. He came into the state, it is said, as a man who regarded his candidacy "with little interest and mild derision." He left it as one who knew he "really had a chance," a "hopeful and aggressive candidate." [6] On such a matter—whether here or there, whether at this point or at that—the calculation can never be proved or disproved beyond all reasonable doubt. For that reason, if for no other, it seems altogether fitting and proper in this place to reaffirm the theory as described above.

Whatever the effect of New Hampshire on Lincoln may have been, his impact on the state is beyond doubt. In January 1860, most Republican leaders were preparing to support either William H. Seward or John C. Fremont. Ten delegates to the Republican convention were selected in April to go to the Wigwam in Chicago. On the first ballot, Maine, the first state on the roll, cast ten votes for Seward and six for Lincoln. New Hampshire, the second state on the roll, cast seven votes for Lincoln, one for Seward, one for Fremont, and one for Salmon P. Chase, who had been born in New Hampshire. At the end of this ballot, Seward led Lincoln by 173½ votes to 102. On the second roll call, New Hampshire cast nine votes for Lincoln, and on the

5. William H. Herndon and Jesse W. Weik, *Life of Lincoln* (Greenwich, Conn.: Fawcett Publications, 1961), pp. 360–361.

6. Richardson, *William E. Chandler*, p. 34.

third and nominating ballot the state voted unanimously for the man who became the next president.

In the election that followed, in November 1860, New Hampshire cast 37,519 votes for Lincoln, 25,881 for Stephen A. Douglas, 2,112 for Breckenridge, and 411 for Bell. In the nation Lincoln received 38 percent of the total vote, in New Hampshire 57 percent. And not long after that, the war, which was foreordained by that election, came.

On April 15, 1861, the president called for 75,000 troops to serve for three months. On May 25, the First New Hampshire Regiment of United States Volunteers was "armed and equipped and ready for the field." They were sent to Washington, where they marched down Pennsylvania Avenue and passed in review before Abraham Lincoln. The president then complimented Colonel Mason Tappan "as having the best and most thoroughly appointed regiment that had thus far reached Washington." [7] The troops were then assigned to picket duty along the Potomac, on the Maryland side of the river.

At that point, the soldiers of New Hampshire entered the legendary stretch of time that runs from Bull Run to Appomattox. Thereafter, they fought on all the hallowed grounds. The Second was in the Peninsula and in the Peach Orchard. The Third was in the Wilderness. The Sixth was at Vicksburg. The Ninth was at Antietam. The Eleventh was at Spotsylvania. The Twelfth was at Chancellorsville. In the twelve months that began with Fair Oaks and ended with Gettysburg, the Fifth fought in the Seven Days' Battle, at Antietam, along Marye's Heights across from Fredericksburg, at Chancellorsville, and at Seminary Ridge. In that time, they lost, in killed, wounded, and missing, about half their original number. In the course of the whole war, there were 2,600 names carried on the roster of the Fifth Regiment and the casualties among them reached 1,500. No other regiment in the Union armies is believed to have suffered such heavy losses. [8]

All told, New Hampshire contributed eighteen regiments of

7. Alonzo J. Fogg, *The Statistics and Gazetteer of New Hampshire* (Concord: P. L. Guernsey, 1874), p. 23.

8. Fogg, *Statistics and Gazetteer*, pp. 24–26.

infantry, a regiment of cavalry, a battery of light artillery, three companies of sharpshooters, and three special units for guard and garrison duty. Three hundred and sixty-six men served in the Marine Corps, and 3,160 served in the United States Navy. The records are neither complete nor precise, but it appears that about 36,000 men were members, at one time or another, of the armed forces—about one in every ten in the population. In the state in 1860 there were 64,406 males between the ages of fifteen and forty. Therefore, almost one man of every two of fighting age served at some time under the colors.

Beneath the statistics lie the particular cases. And in a state where the largest city, Manchester, had a population of 20,068 and the smallest community, Odell's Township, had one resident, the particular case had special weight. The fact that every other man in the prime of life went off to fight was felt in the school room, in the congregation, on the farm, in the mill, around the hearth, and among the neighbors. The war that took place 400 miles and more away became a local thing, a part of the day's experience, what families lived with, what sons did.

All that is now left of that war in many towns says as much. The remaining evidence is, often, the work of a man named Martin Milmore. He was a sculptor who had produced great statues of senators, generals, philosophers, and popes. For several states, he also had produced great structures of marble and metal in memory of those who died in battle. His grand monuments, it was said, "were among the best of their time." [9] What he made for New Hampshire towns can still be seen in small parks and on village greens. It is the figure, cast in bronze, of a single man in the uniform of a Union infantryman. He stands, right foot slightly to the rear, head bent slightly forward, hands—breast high—holding the barrel of his rifle, in the position of parade rest. The effect is not so much militant as reflective, not so much monumental as personal.

9. *Dictionary of American Biography*, 13:18.

13

Change

IN 1874, there were 893 miles of railway track in the state. It was claimed that "nearly every hamlet . . . can hear the clarion sound of the locomotive and see the white, curling smoke as it hovers o'er the track of the swiftly passing train." [1] If this was not entirely true, it was true enough. Any traveller prepared to take the considerable trouble required to obtain separate tickets from each of the thirty-two companies that owned the railroads could, in time, get pretty much around the whole state. What he would see from the car windows on such a trip would lead him to conclude, in all probability, that all the pieces shaken loose by the war had been nicely put together again.

If he were like most other travellers in the state the first thing that would strike his eye would be the unchanging landmarks. From the beginning, there was a tendency to speak of them in the superlative. The eighteen miles of seacoast are the finest on the New England Atlantic coast. No alp is "more fabled" than Chocorua. Near Lancaster, the Connecticut River "winds round a succession of the richest and most gracefully formed intervales in a manner unexampled. Handsomer and richer lands probably do not exist." A man who claimed to have seen almost everything in the Western world asserted that there was nothing any-

1. Fogg, *Statistics and Gazetteer*, p. 409.

where to equal the view northward from Alton Bay. And farther to the north lay the great range, those Crystal Hills of early times, where countless visitors through the years "felt that the beautiful and sublime were here mingled upon a scale never to be surpassed." In sum, "there is no doubt but the scenery of New Hampshire is more varied and beautiful than can be found in any other state in the Union." [2]

In search of practical grades and the shortest lines that could be constructed with due regard for economy between any two points, the railroads often passed through more ordinary landscapes. There are, in fact—especially in the southern half of the state—extensive reaches of low-lying, swampy land and recurring stands of scrub pine and spruce. Of necessity, the trains spent a certain amount of time making their way through such flat and, at times, forlorn terrain. But then the rights of way would lead into small, winding river valleys and among low-lying, rolling hills. In this country, a traveller in 1874 would have looked out upon the classic scenes—cattle and sheep in rocky pastures; plowed ground; the small white house framed by elms, flecked here and there by the color of rose and lilac; the large grey barns. And then, somewhat farther on, at intervals of eight or ten miles, the towns: steeples against the sky, clusters of white clapboard, public buildings of brick or granite facing, the water-powered mills for textiles, the factories making all kinds of things out of wood. These were the small towns that fitted naturally into the natural surroundings, centers of agricultural activity and the supporting works of industry. Everything in 1874, as seen from a train window, appeared in satisfying scale, proportion, and balance. The peacefulness of the landscape was matched by what the *Gazetteer* called "the *busy* quiet in our fields, our workshops and our mercantile streets." [3]

Certain statistics supported the appearances. Engaged in farming were 46,593 people, who produced farm products

2. Fogg, *Statistics and Gazetteer*, p. 180; Timothy Dwight, *Travels in New England and New York*, edited by Barbara M. Solomon, 4 vols. (Cambridge, Mass.: Harvard University Press, 1969), 2:94; Fogg, *Statistics and Gazetteer*, p. 561; *New Hampshire, A Guide to the Granite State* (Boston: Houghton Mifflin Company, 1938), p. 5.

3. Fogg, *Statistics and Gazetteer*, p. 39.

worth \$22,473,547 in 1874. About the same number were in manufacturing; 31,405 males and 16,667 females for a total of 48,072. They made 148 different kinds of things—from barrels and books and hats to artificial limbs, coffins, cheese, shoes, pianos, and elastic sponges. In fact, almost everything a citizen needed in the course of a day—household requirements, working equipment, and diversionary mechanisms—were made in his own state.

There are, however, other statistics which indicate that things were not always what they seemed to the casual traveller. The facts of life—which for twenty years had been veiled behind the claims of habit, the attachments of memory, and the sentimental rhetoric of party leaders—had begun by 1870, to make themselves both visible and felt. There was first the grim figure in the census of that year. During the previous decade the United States as a whole had increased in population by 26 percent while New Hampshire's population, for the first time in its history, had decreased by 2 percent. From the beginning, there had been the tendency for native sons to go elsewhere to seek their fortunes. As Abraham Lincoln had said, New Hampshire—like Maryland—was a good state to come from. It had, in fact, been a source of pride that, from this small community men like Daniel Webster, Charles A. Dana, Salmon P. Chase, Horace Greeley, Lewis Cass, and Jonas Chickering had gone forth to serve with distinction in other parts of the nation and in all walks of life. But by 1870 it was clear that what had been a tendency among the more restive in the population had become a settled and general condition.

In that year, there were 124,979 persons, born within the boundaries, who were living elsewhere in the country. Brooding on these figures, Alonzo Fogg, compiler of *The Statistics and Gazetteer of New Hampshire,* concluded that there had never been anything like it in any state or nation this side of Ireland. Thoughtful men, he said, should consider "that the Natives of New Hampshire can truly be classed with the lone Indian, for with a loss at the same ratio [as 1870]for the next fifty years, not a vestige of pure, original New Hampshire blood will be left that ran in the veins of our forefathers one hundred years ago." [4]

Other states, if not nations, had in fact been subjected to the same sobering conditions. They were, for the most part, New England neighbors. As early as 1857, Professor J. W. Patterson had told the Grafton County Agricultural Society that in that very season 300,000 men and women had moved from the hillsides and valleys of New England to other parts of the country. The causes of this exodus were several. To begin with, there was that sense, which in these years developed the pulling power of a myth, that the course of empire lay westward. There was also, in these years and in all the following years of the century, what was called, not incorrectly, the lure of the city. To these impalpable sources of attraction was added the force of indisputable fact. New England, and especially New Hampshire, was not as good a place for farmers as it once had been. As soon as the rich soil of the Middle West was opened up, it could be seen that the rocky ground of the state had only marginal utility. Furthermore, the favorable conditions of the Middle West enabled men to develop, in time, a different kind of farming in which crops for sale drove out the thought of simply growing things for the subsistence of the farmer and his family.

All of these factors combined to draw people away from New Hampshire, and most of those who left came off the farms. In 1840, half the ground within the state's boundaries had been cultivated land, but by 1870 only 39 percent was so designated, and in each remaining decade of the century this percentage was further reduced. As time passed, the landscape increasingly revealed the marks of this long, slow decline. A French visitor in the later years of the period noticed "sloven farms [that] alternate with vast areas of territory, half forest, half pasturage; farm buildings partly in ruins." [5] And in the final stage, there were the great grey piles of barns collapsed; the heaps of red brick;

4. Fogg, *Statistics and Gazetteer*, p. 453.
5. Arthur M. Schlesinger, *The Rise of the City* (New York: The Macmillan Company, 1933), p. 68.

the cellar holes choked with alder; the elms or maples in brush-filled dooryards and, in season, a rose in bloom.

In the days when farming had been a way of life, the towns that had grown up to supply the goods and services required by the local farmers had developed their own peculiar character. Together, the farm and the town had determined the quality of life within the state. As men and women left their rural homesteads in ever greater numbers, the effect was inevitably felt within the towns themselves. At the same time, these towns were subjected to the presence of a new force, more subtle but more powerful than simple loss of the surrounding farm population.

The nature of this new force might have been indistinctly perceived by the casual traveller in 1874, but he would have had no way to calculate its ultimate consequences. On the surface, things seemed about the way they had always been. The town of Stoddard is a good example. It is a hill town in Cheshire County. Some of the houses are so placed that rain falling on one side of the roofs drains down to the Connecticut River, while the rain that falls on the other side runs off to the Merrimack. The soil in the township is "deep with a clay bottom. As cold and moisture are its predominant qualities [it] is better adapted to grazing than tillage." Its hills and fourteen ponds give the town a most attractive surrounding. As far back as 1820, the farmers had produced impressive quantities of agricultural products in a year—32,000 pounds of butter, 71,000 pounds of beef, 85,000 pounds of pork, 5,700 pounds of flax and 600 barrels of cider. Fifty years later "agriculture [was] still the principal employment of the people." But considerable manufacturing had developed: "30,000 shingles and 700,000 feet of boards are sawed annually. Glass bottles to the value of $40,000 are manufactured. 80,000 tubs and pails and 17,000 boxes of clothes pins are annually made. Granite of a fine quality is wrought to a considerable extent." [6]

By all of the obvious measurements of the time save one, Stoddard would seem, in 1874, to have been a model of that

6. Fogg, *Statistics and Gazetteer*, p. 338.

desired balance between farming and diversified small industry upon which the society rested. In 1820 its population had been 1,203; in 1870 its population was 663. Three hundred people had left in the previous decade.

Off to the north in Coos County lies the town of Whitefield. The soil here is good and, in 1874, farming was important, but the big thing was the lumber business—and the biggest thing in that business was A. L. and W. G. Brown & Co. The Messrs. Brown had a mill 250 feet long and 160 feet wide, powered by three steam engines supplemented by water power. A railroad ran alongside the mill building to a platform, where lumber was loaded directly into the cars to be taken to Boston.

In the mill, where 120 men worked, there were two circular saws, three shingle machines, two power edgers, four planers, two trimming saws, a groover, and two slab saws. Each day this mill made, among other things, 14,000 shingles and 40,000 feet of lumber. In a year it produced 10.5 million lathes, 4.2 million shingles, 12 million feet of long timber, and 300,000 clapboards.

To achieve this production "the labor is all done in a systematic plan, and everything connected with the mill, from the rolling of the logs into the pond, to the loading of the lumber on the cars for its final destination, moves like clockwork. Every man knows his place and duty, and is held responsible for doing his part of the work when offered to him and delivering it to the next man, when required." [7] The town in which all this activity took place had housed 281 people in 1820; in 1870 the population was 1,196. Two hundred men and women had been added to the community in the previous ten years.

In the differences between Stoddard and Whitefield can be found most of the factors that were to determine the history of New Hampshire for many years to come. For one thing, the people of Stoddard did not have at their disposal any particularly significant single resource; they made, as their fathers had, small quantities of things from the materials they could find in the immediate vicinity—some wood, some granite, some flax,

7. Fogg, *Statistics and Gazetteer*, p. 369.

some clay. Whitefield, on the other hand, was surrounded by one of the greatest stands of timber to be found in the whole country. Then there was the railroad. Men in Stoddard could reach it by taking the stage fifteen miles to Keene or sixteen miles to Peterborough. In Whitefield, the tracks ran right through the town, out to the lumber mills, and on to the adjacent timber fields. Finally, there was the difference in the way six men in Stoddard made 30,000 shingles in a year and the way 120 men in Whitefield made the same number in two days. There was at work in Whitefield that "systematic plan" within which every man knew his own place and duty and was held responsible for doing his part of the work when offered to him.

That plan, first developed in the early textile mills, spread slowly as a way of organizing human energy. But after the Civil War, gathering momentum, it increasingly supplied the pattern for the way men made things—all kinds of things. The great advantage of this systematic plan was that men working within it could make boxes, or stoves, or cutter bars, or wheels that were exactly alike, in great quantity and at small cost. In time, not only more and more men but more and more machines—from saws and planers to shapers and gear cutters and lathes and drills, all power driven—were brought into the systematic plan. Most of the history of this country since the Civil War can be written as an expression of what happens when things are made this way.

What happened in many towns in New Hampshire was that the residents discovered they could not fit into the systematic plan. Like Stoddard, these communities lacked sufficient raw materials, adequate transport, the necessary capital, and the required labor supply. They lost ground, population, and energy and some of them disappeared altogether. For ever-lengthening years, the men and women in these communities conducted an often resourceful but always dwindling rearguard action to protect the existence of those farms and towns which had for so long determined the quality of New Hampshire life.

Some industries, notably textiles, and some communities found it possible to accommodate more easily to the new conditions. All around the state in the last half of the century long-settled places like Claremont, Keene, Nashua, Somersworth, Dover, Exeter, Lebanon, evolved slowly into something between a village and a city—the gathering of ten, fifteen, twenty thousand people into the familiar type—the New England mill town.

Within this slow drift of things there was, in the southern part of the state, one astounding exception. "The record of the real Manchester," said its historian in 1874, "is little more, for a time at least, than the record of its manufacturing." [8] In this sense, it was more like those other American cities that owed their existence to the new systematic plan of making things than it was like the other communities in its own state. As it was with rubber and Akron, steel and Pittsburgh, glass and Muncie, wheat and Minneapolis, so it was with cloth and Manchester. Because Manchester fitted so naturally and significantly into the developing national scheme in the second half of the last century, it is worth some special notice.

Those mills built in the 1830s and 1840s were steadily added to in the years that followed. By the 1880s they extended in dark grandeur about three miles along the east side of the Merrimack River like some great rampart. The continuous line of red brick along the water was, in fact, the west wall of a dense and complicated network of mill structures that, threaded by narrow and tortuous passages, extended well inland. The whole was a huge mass, impossible to comprehend in its entirety with the eye from any single point. But it had, and still has, a kind of satisfying, if monumental, scale and proportion throughout. Nearby, really a self-evident part of the same scheme, were the row houses, the tenements, the boarding houses built—for the most part, like the mills—of brick by the Amoskeag Manufacturing Company for its employees. These were extensive structures. At the height of its prosperity near the end of the nineteenth century, the Amoskeag mills and associated industries employed 15,000 people. That was more people than there were in any town or city in the rest of the state.

This massive enterprise had evolved in the years since 1837

---

8. Clarke, *Manchester*, p. 267.

in an interesting way. There was first the matter of simple addition—one great new building after another for the spinning, weaving, and dyeing of cloth as demand increased around the world. Then there was the matter of variation. Near the beginning, in 1840, shops had been built for the construction of the machinery to be used in the expanding mills. Two years later, a foundry was put in and six years after that another foundry was added. During the first decade, the men who worked in these installations learned the new art of making nicely fitting machinery out of iron and steel under factory conditions. During the same decade, negotiations were completed for the building of the Northern Railroad from Concord to White River Junction. One of the things a railway needs is locomotives, but no one in the country knew how to build them very well in those days. So it was natural for the owners of the railroad to turn to the shops of the Amoskeag Manufacturing Company, where the labor force had acquired considerable experience in making heavy machinery. In 1849, the first locomotive in Manchester was put together. During the next ten years, the shops built 231 more engines for various railroads throughout the country.

From what was learned in this undertaking a further step naturally followed. In 1859, the company started building steam fire engines. These engines, in the years immediately following, were manufactured with increasing sophistication and in great number—engines of the first and second class, engines with single and double pump, even self-propellers that did away with the need for horses. They were sold everywhere in the United States, and in such faraway places as England, Russia China, Peru, and New South Wales.

As time passed, these shops acquired the machines, tools, instruments, and skilled labor needed to make almost all the parts—turbines, boilers, stationary engines, flywheels, belting, gear boxes and so forth—required by a developing and expanding industrial economy. During the war, they made Springfield rifles, sewing machines to fabricate uniforms for the Union army, and turned out the great brass rings on which the gun turrets of the *Monitor* rode.

After the war, the cardinal principle enunciated by Andrew

Carnegie (put all your eggs in one basket, and watch the basket)—that is, specialization—began to dominate American industry. Particular companies began to make particular things—locomotives, turbines, brass rings, stationary engines. By 1876, the Amoskeag Manufacturing Company had begun to concentrate its energies and skills on its own eggs—the making of cotton cloth in great quantity. In the closing years of the century, it proceeded, like some force of nature, to become the greatest single manufacturer of cotton cloth in the world—producing one mile of material a minute.

The power to operate the machinery came, in the first years, from wheels turned by the water in the Amoskeag falls. In 1883, steam engines supplemented this original source, and in 1896, electric motors supplied the additional needs for energy. The native Americans who worked the machinery had originally come from the surrounding farms—some men and more young girls. Then in 1840, a woman who had been born in Ireland started work at the Amoskeag, and in the years that followed, she was joined by many others who had been born in many different countries. By the end of the century, the names on the payroll were Irish, English, French, German, Scotch, Swedish, Russian, Greek. By far the greatest number, the majority in any given year, were from French Canada. They began coming into the city in 1840 and continued the steady flow of immigration throughout the remainder of the century. Whatever the total number of this work force at any given time—5,000, 10,000, 12,000, 17,000 are sometimes given as the maximums—in later years the percentage of males to females remained fairly constant at about one in three.

Especially in the early years, many of these operatives, as they were called, lived in housing built for them by the company or in houses sold to them by the company. They worked on schedules that were gradually reduced through the years. By 1905, the day began at 6:30 A.M. and ended, after a free hour at noon, at 6:00 P.M. Saturday afternoon and Sunday were times of freedom. The total work week was fifty-eight hours—a fairly normal working schedule in this country at the time. Some, as in the building trades, worked less and some, as in the iron trade, worked harder. (In Pittsburgh, in the first decade of the century, 34,000 men worked twelve-hour shifts seven days a week.)

It was not a time when, by today's standards, either the conditions or the rewards of factory labor were attractive. The people who worked in the Amoskeag were certainly no worse off—and were probably a bit better off—than those who worked in industry elsewhere. Just as it is difficult from available records to get a clear idea of average pay scales, or—in view of the radical changes in the value of money—to obtain an understanding of the purchasing power of a day's work in those days, so it is difficult to discover any good measurement for the levels of discontent or contentment in the mills. About all one can say is that, while wages and hours by today's standards seem scarcely bearable, work in the textile industry was safer and cleaner than in many other branches of American industry at the time, and that, at the Amoskeag mills, particular care was taken to avoid accidents. Over the years, there were very few bad or fatal occasions. As far as management was concerned, it seemed that the men and women on their payroll were on the whole sober, hard-working, courteous, intelligent human beings. And given the prevailing conditions and pressures of American industrial development at the time, the managers made an effort to respond in kind.

The specific arts of management in Manchester were more demanding of character than of mind or imagination. When Andrew Jackson visited the mills in the early days he had said to Samuel Slater, who accompanied him: "You set all those spindles in motion . . . so that we may become an industrial people." To which Slater replied: "If it please you, sir, I suppose I did give out the psalm, and they have been singing to the tune ever since." [9] For years thereafter, those who made cotton proceeded in accordance with words and music that were, on the whole, unchanging. The problem in the mills was to insure the proper regulation of repeating procedures, and to supervise the extension of those procedures to increase production. What

9. George W. Browne, *The Amoskeag Manufacturing Company of Manchester, New Hampshire* (Manchester, N.H.: Amoskeag Manufacturing Company, 1915), p. 56.

was needed in this kind of management was firmness, fairness, clarity of purpose, commitment to the task, a due regard for the legitimate claims of human beings, and an understanding of the interests of the owners.

Ezekiel Albert Straw possessed all these qualities. Born in Salisbury, New Hampshire, educated in the English Department of Phillips Academy at Andover, he had come—as a boy of nineteen, and almost by accident—to the Amoskeag mills in 1838. During the next ten years, he learned everything there was to know about making cloth, from the construction of a dam to the placing of a loom. In 1844, he went to England and "brought back from the manufactories into which he gained access on one pretext and another" the secrets of making and printing muslin delaines. From the knowledge thus acquired, he supervised the building of the Manchester print works, the first manufactories of delaines in this country. Twelve years later, he was made the agent for the owners and thus became the manager responsible for all the company works in Manchester. He also became a leading citizen of the city and, in time, a power in the politics of the state. From 1872 to 1874 he was governor of New Hampshire. Hard working, calm, public-spirited, faithful to "his ideas of what is right" and "liberal in his gifts to the poor and all charitable institutions," to him more than any other man who lived in the city, it was generally agreed, Manchester was indebted for its great prosperity. He served as agent from 1856 to 1878. Seven years later, his son Herman F. Straw assumed the post, to be followed about twenty years later by his grandson William Parker Straw. From the beginning to the end, the Straw family had a direct hand in the supervision of the operations of the Amoskeag Manufacturing Company.[10]

Similar continuity was reflected in the persons of those who controlled the larger fortunes of the company. Five of the six men on the board of directors in 1908 could trace connections— by blood, marriage, or ancient association—to predecessors who had come on the board in the crucial year of 1837. Most of them, in fact, could claim connection with the Lyman mills in

10. Clarke, *Manchester,* p. 435.

Waltham, where Francis Lowell and Nathan Appleton had
started it all in 1812. The paths that brought and held them all
together were as extensive and intricate as those which tied all
their mill buildings together along the banks of the Merrimack.

By the end of the nineteenth century, the men in control were
considerably removed by interest and occupation from the actual
processes of making and selling cloth. The mills were a single
contingency in the varied affairs—social, cultural, political, and
most of all financial—that commanded their attention. Then,
too, they lived in Boston, or near it, where lay the center of
gravity for their active, well-ordered lives. The stewardship
supplied by these men and their ancestors in the nineteenth century determined not only the fortunes of the mills, but the character of Manchester as well. According to the *Gazetteer* in
1874:

> The Amoskeag is the largest, and most powerful corporation in the
> State, and while it has always looked at the main chance (or their
> own interest) it has always looked at the best interest of the city. For
> (what is termed) a soul-less institution, it has been very liberal in its
> donations.[11]

These remarks are not only circumspect but also contain a
sort of measured truth. From the beginning, it will be recalled,
the intent was to create surroundings in mill and city which
would be as favorable as possible for both working and living.
The plan for Manchester as drawn up in 1837 contained many
reserved areas for public squares, parks, lawns, and charming
ponds. It also contained a rational plan for the organization of
streets and sections. The spirit of these plans was faithfully preserved by the man who became treasurer of the company in
1837. William Amory was the son of a Boston merchant, a
graduate of Harvard, a student of law in Göttingen and of literature in Berlin. He was the Amoskeag treasurer for more than
forty years and in that time he, more than any other, made
Manchester a city of wide streets, pleasant squares, and gracious parks. He also saw to it that the company made proper
place for, and contributed to, the construction of public build-

11. Fogg, *Statistics and Gazetteer*, p. 239.

ings and made land available on easy terms for private dwellings.

But neither the force of original intent nor the faithful ministrations of able men in the service of that intent could wholly control the shape and direction of events. Manchester, like other cities, was forced into existence and rapid growth by the amazing industrial development of the last half of the nineteenth century. It, like them, was subject to all the pressures created by the energy that was attracted to the main chance—in this case the making of cotton goods. The life of the city was determined by the work of the mills. Those who worked there were drawn, increasingly as time went on and demand went up, from other places and other cultures. They all tended to keep their distance from one another. By far the largest, and in many ways the most important group, the French Canadians, tended to set up their own society—separate parishes, separate schools, separate newspapers, separate clubs. Accordingly, the interesting differences of this group were not transferred, along with the differences among the other groups, into any kind of cosmopolitan whole. The city of Manchester, the principal source of energy in the state, exerted its influence only in things that could be measured and counted—horsepower, spindles, payrolls, yards of cloth, bank deposits, votes, taxes, profits. In all these matters, within the normal context of life around the state, it was extraordinary. Even more extraordinary—after the payrolls had been met and the local taxes paid—were the profits. Most of these flowed over the border, usually to Massachusetts, and most of all into the hands of a few people in Boston, who, as the years went by, knew less and less about the making of cotton cloth, not much about Manchester, and almost nothing about the needs of New Hampshire.

One hundred and twenty miles due north of Manchester, in the last half of the nineteenth century, another industry—in fact, a whole society—was developing that was also not much like anything else to be found in the state. From the far end of the White Mountains to the bleak land around and beyond the Connecticut lakes there was a great reach of "heavy, unbroken forest of spruce and balsam fir, together with some hemlock, cedar, and hardwood." [12] This was the North Country—Coos County—where, since 1825, there had been continuous small logging operations. In the years after the Civil War, these operations were increasingly consolidated under the control of the Berlin Mills Company, which later became the Brown Company. By the end of the century this company owned 360,000 acres in Maine, Vermont, and New Hampshire. In later years its total holdings in these three states and Canada came to 3,750,000 acres or 6,000 square miles—somewhat larger than the state of Connecticut.

After the Civil War, there was much in the lumber business that followed the new systematic plan for making things, as in the operations at Whitefield already described. In time, the Brown Company expanded its activities to include the making of paper and pulp. Then, to the rational plan for organizing large scale production was added the final and most sophisticated element in the developing American industry, the industrial research laboratory that looked in a systematic way for new uses for wood, and thus for new products.

The management of the Brown Company, passing from father to son, was thoroughly familiar with the nature of lumbering operations, skilled in negotiation, and enlightened in its preparation for the future. The research laboratory founded in 1913 was one of the first in any industry in this country. And, from 1890 onwards, the members of the company were devoted to the principles of sensible forest management. They played a considerable part in the development by the state of wise conservation programs. In almost all ways they represented modern industrial methods. But in one area of operations, for most of the last half of the nineteenth century, those methods seemed not so much like those of Manchester or Pittsburgh as like those used in the old mast trade 150 years before. The trees were cut down by hand, brought on horse-drawn skids along rough roads "swamped out" through the forest to the waterside, and then floated down the wild spring floods to the mills. At every point

12. William R. Brown, *Our Forest Heritage* (Concord, N.H.: The New Hampshire Historical Society, 1958), p. 13.

of the process there was a need for special skills, and at many points there was intruding danger.

The work was done by crews who spent much of their lives in the forest, at zero temperatures and in three feet of snow. They lived in camps—thirty-five to forty-five at any given time spread through the huge silent terrain—miles from town or city. Where men in factories used up 3,000 calories a day, a man in the woods needed 7,000 calories. He obtained this fuel by eating—every day—beans, peas, flour, salt pork, molasses, dried apples, potatoes, pilot bread, and tea or canned milk.

To work in the woods put a man about as close to direct, hand-to-hand encounters with the forces of nature as one could get in those days, and the work put anyone closer in spirit to the settlers who had first come to fish and look for furs than to those who were working in the factories of Nashua, Manchester, or Lebanon. What came out of it was a particular kind of person: tough, independent, skilled, resourceful, jocose, totally taken up with the job to be done, set apart from others by that job and experience. There was more direct connection between cause and effect, more wildness and freedom, than could be found in most other ways to make a living in this country.

The "capital" of this area—and of this society—was Berlin. Most of the logs brought down the Androscoggin in the great drives ended up in the red brick mills on the western bank of the river near the falls. It was, therefore, in some ways, a city of smoking factories even in the early days. But it was also a frontier town to which those who had spent months in the woods were drawn, not so much for rest as for recreation. Shut off to the south by the White Mountains and on the east, west, and north by unbroken forests, Berlin developed a boisterous, varied life of its own. Much of its variety was supplied by the different nationalities that had been attracted to the special conditions—French Canadians, Norwegians, Germans, and, eventually, Russians. During the nineteenth century, most of these ethnic groups kept to themselves—in Irish Acre, German Town, Little Canada, or Norwegian Village. In the churches, services were conducted in five different languages.

But since the town was small—8,000 in 1897—each of these

groups made itself felt in interesting ways. The Norwegians started the oldest skiing club in the country, the French Canadians brought in ice hockey before the rest of the country knew much about the game, and took over the town with dramatic processions at the annual Feast of St. John. Taken all together with its diverse population, its controlling influence in one of the principal industries of the state, and its place as a center of energy in the middle of nowhere, it was a community arrestingly different from all others in the state.

14

Summer People

T is interesting that these concentrations of developing enterprise—the North Country and Manchester—did not operate with more determining effect upon what may be called the state of mind of New Hampshire during the last fifty years of the nineteenth century. The same thing could be said for growing towns like Claremont, Lebanon, Somersworth, Dover, or Nashua which in these years became centers of diversified industry. The state seemed to others—and to itself—still a place of small villages, small farms, and pastoral landscapes. Much energy, in fact, was expended during this period to support this scheme of things against the intruding forces of change. In 1870, the Board of Agriculture was established by the state to put farmers in touch with the most modern methods of cultivation, cropping, feeding, and fertilizing. Somewhat later, the first chapter of the Patrons of Husbandry—the Grange—was started in Exeter. The influence of this organization—agricultural, social, political, and financial—soon spread throughout the state. It was for a long time the dominant institution in the lives of farmers and the development of agriculture.

Both these agencies, the Board and the Grange, played a leading part in the shift of interest and practice that occurred on New Hampshire farms in these years. When, before the Civil War, it had become apparent that the small, diversified subsistence farm was no longer an effective unit, the increasingly successful move to raise sheep began. Starting in 1812, when the famous Merino stock was introduced from Spain, the number of sheep had grown steadily in the state until, in 1840, more than 600,000 were on the hillside pastures. In later years, the wool schedules of the tariffs and the competition from western flocks steadily reduced the possibility of growing sheep successfully in the state, and the number of flocks dwindled steadily throughout the Civil War. In the 1870s, it was necessary to find a profitable substitute, and the shift was made to dairy herds. The development of the railroads coincided with the increasing concentration on dairy products, and the milk trains to Boston and other urban centers made this a profitable business for several decades.

But, as time passed it became obvious that the way New Hampshire could best live off the land was not so much by growing things on it as by attracting people to it. In its very first report, the Board of Agriculture had called attention to the fact that—while the mountains, hills, rocky pastures, stony fields, and countless ponds and small lakes were not promising terrain for growing things—they nevertheless were a natural resource that could be used in another kind of trade. Since the beginning, of course, men and women had come casually and occasionally into the state to seek pleasure and repose in the beauty of its natural surroundings. But after the Civil War, there developed those organized and contrived visitations that the improved transport and the higher standard of living of the visitors made possible—and the economic uncertainties of the state made necessary. There was considerable variety in the form of these activities.

To begin with, there was the farmhouse for three or four "summer boarders." School teachers, librarians, clerks, and widows or widowers with a little laid by would come for a week or two to live with a farmer's family. They would eat the fresh farm food prepared by the farmer's wife, walk down to the small pool in the nearby brook, sit on the porch in the rocking chairs to look at the sun as it struck the hills across the neighboring meadow. Every now and then, the farmer would hitch the team to the Democrat (a kind of light wagon with two seats) and drive his guests to some special point of interest for a picnic lunch. But mostly they just stayed within their comfortable, simple, friendly surroundings and sat in those rockers to, as they said, invite the soul.

Then there were the summer hotels. Most of these were simple, straightforward establishments built near a pond and a view. Usually, they were constructed of wood, contained thirty or forty large bedrooms, and, on the ground floor, offered public rooms that were large, well-proportioned, and crammed with heavy, comfortable furniture. The food was honest and substantial.

Away to the north, there was a different kind of hotel and a different sort of visitor. At strategic points throughout the White Mountains, there were great rambling structures—the Glen House, the Crawford House, the Kearsarge House, the Mount Washington Hotel—designed to support those seeking to contemplate the grandeur of nature with a splendor appropriate to their surroundings. Excellent food; ornate furniture; well-tended gardens; thoughtful service; carefully organized excursions to places of interest—the Flume, the Notches, the Old Man of the Mountain—were all put within easy reach of the men and women who came in by the cars from Boston or on the sleepers from New York. Life in these sumptuous resorts was not unlike life in one of the European health spas and watering places, where a principal reviving agent lay in the seeing and the being seen.

> The Kearsarge House is a new and elegant hotel, erected during the year 1872 and has accommodation for three hundred guests. It is delightfully located in the very heart of the village, and commands fine views in all directions. A fine band of music is engaged for each season, and with a daily arrival of one hundred to one hundred and fifty persons, a lively and animated scene is presented at all times of the day and evening, for in addition to its own guests, it is made an exchange or center where guests from other hotels, are sure to meet friends who are either stopping temporarily or passing through the place on their way to the mountains.[1]

There were other kinds of visitors, less well-heeled, perhaps, but surer-footed, who came to the same area in increasing

1. Fogg, *Statistics and Gazetteer*, p. 121.

numbers in these years. They stayed in smaller establishments, putting up by night in one of the numerous inns or farm houses, and going forth by day to walk along a steadily enlarging network of trails and to climb the more rugged mountains. In time, the marvelous tract of land from the northern slopes of the great range to Wolfeboro on the southern shore of Lake Winnipesaukee became a place for the summer restoration of all sorts and conditions of people. They came to get away from whatever it was they were doing—to lose or find or refresh themselves in surroundings that nature and man had conspired to make welcoming, gracious, and lovely.

Then there was the "summer place," the piece of property bought by people—usually out-of-staters—who returned each succeeding summer for several months. In the 1880s and 1890s, these places were often the farmlands and farmhouses left behind by the men and women who had gone West or to the city to seek an easier and perhaps larger fortune. The price for such properties was not only right, it was ordinarily so low that very attractive sites and structures were available to those with modest means. Ministers, college professors, doctors, independent small businessmen, professional people of all kinds discovered that they could find and afford just the sort of view, just the sort of wooded acreage, just the sort of small house with character they wanted for their vacations. Their search was often assisted by the Board of Agriculture, which furnished lists and descriptions of abandoned properties. So successful was the promotion, so great was the attraction, that, in the first years of the new century, more land in some areas was owned by people from other places than by local residents.

Not all these new vacationers—summer people—settled on the old farmland and in the old farm houses. A good many built small, cheap, dull cottages that rimmed the shores of countless small lakes and ponds. Others built, by the side of their own ponds or on top of their own hillsides, what the people of the period thought of as mansions—great structures sheathed in brown shingles, containing high-studded living rooms with massive field-stone fireplaces, alcoves, servants' quarters, porte-cocheres, and numberless porches or piazzas for the views. As time went on, some of the more imposing buildings of this type were to be found, as they often are, along the seaboard—at Hampton, Little Boar's Head, and Rye Beach. These estates, as they were called—with their grand houses, attractive gardens, gleaming lawns and shade trees—added a kind of splendor to the natural setting which has been described as the finest on the North Atlantic Coast.

Not all those who came into the state sought simple diversion or relaxation from the cares of their world. Some were attracted because New Hampshire seemed to offer favorable environment for painting, composing music, writing. As early as 1850, Benjamin Champney had discovered that North Conway was an interesting place to paint. He had been born in New Ipswich and had entered the world of art by a series of improbable circumstances that led in time to the study of painting in Paris and then on the banks of the Rhine. Both in France and in Germany, Champney went directly to nature for his subjects, which put him a little ahead of his time.

It was this concern for landscape that drew him, in due course, to North Conway, and it was both his ability and his pleasant personality that induced others to follow him there. "By 1853," he said, "the meadows and banks of the Saco were dotted all about with white umbrellas." [2] Beneath the parasols were such men as John Kensett, Thomas Cole, Albert Bierstadt, and George Innes. If, in their diversity of mood and collective influence, they were not quite so distinctive as a White Mountain School, as they were sometimes called, they were certainly, in their number and association, an art colony—the first of several that developed in the state in the second half of the century. More enduring and famous than North Conway was the community that started when sculptor Augustus Saint-Gaudens bought a large brick house and plenty of land to go with it in Cornish for $500. Saint-Gaudens was a city man, reared in New York—a familiar in Rome and Paris when he came to New Hampshire. He was not at all sure he would like it, but he did—so much, in fact, that it became a central influence in his

2. *Dictionary of American Biography*, 3:610.

life and in the lives of many who followed him there: Charles Platt, Maud Howe Elliott, Thomas Dewing, Louise Homer, Winston Churchill, Frederick MacMonnies, Kenyon Cox, Herbert Adams, George de Forest Brush. In time, almost everybody who was anybody in the field of the arts came to Cornish—for a night, a weekend, or a week. And also, of course, the rich and great and the merely rich were eventually attracted to this place to build their summer homes, brush up against the cultural emanations, fill the coffers of the local stores and livery stables, and drive the price of real estate upward.

Something of the same sort happened later to the east in Dublin, where Abbott Thayer, Joseph Lindon Smith, Alexander James, Richard Merryman, and George de Forest Brush of the Cornish group stuck to their painting as a conventional society of summer residents from St. Louis, Boston, and New York grew up around them. Farther east, and still later, a more carefully planned and organized sanctuary for artists was established at the MacDowell Colony in Peterborough.

What is one to make of all these exotic exercises—the writing of poems, the painting of pictures, the carving of statues, the playing of music—on abandoned hillside pastures and in reconstructed farm houses? For one thing, New Hampshire, better than most places, supplied what were then understood to be some of the essential conditions for the play of the artistic imagination. It was a time when many believed that art survived only in separation from both the humdrum and the frantic in everyday life. And, indeed, in that time the central energy of industrial development in the country seemed to drive out concern for all goods and services that could not directly support further industrial development. It was a bad season for artists, and in New Hampshire they could find sanctuary from the world of the Philistines who got and spent where populations were doubling every ten years. In fact, the principle of insulation worked—some of the best things Saint-Gaudens ever did were made in New Hampshire; some of the best pictures painted by Abbott Thayer, some of the best novels written by Winston Churchill, and, later, some of the best poetry and fiction written by E. A. Robinson, Thornton Wilder, and Willa Cather were conceived and executed at one or another of these centers of artistic energy in the state.

If much that was done seems at this remove wanting somewhat in force and original perception, that is not much to the point. Whatever many artists found they had to say they said best in New Hampshire, or with the conditions offered by the state in mind. For instance, some years after Saint-Gaudens had come to Cornish, Paul Elmer More quit his teaching of classical literature and went to Shelburne. This was a village in the North Country, on the banks of the Androscoggin, "full of grand mountain scenery" where several writers had gathered in a small, casual colony. More reached this isolated spot by way of St. Louis, Missouri, Cambridge, Massachusetts, and Bryn Mawr, Pennsylvania. To those who had known him in these places, he was "companionable, witty, urbane and suave." In Shelburne, he withdrew for two years into a life of study and meditation. Emerging around the turn of the century, he entered upon a life of reading, teaching, and writing that produced what has been called "the most ambitious and often the most penetrating body of judicial literary criticism in our literature." In the years from 1904 to 1921, this body of learning was published in a series of eleven volumes to which More gave the general title *The Shelburne Essays*. Having left the village behind him, his work thereafter retained, says a biographer, "a spirit of calm detachment of which Shelburne came to be a sort of symbol." [3]

What such small bits of evidence can be made to signify is anybody's guess. It may suggest that New Hampshire, especially those parts of it that in earlier days sustained a special kind of country life, had, in the days of its decline—and perhaps even because of its decline—offered certain kinds of people opportunities they could not find elsewhere. These opportunities had to do with matters of scale; physical dimension; specificity of cause and effect in human concerns; directness of certain kinds of experience; particularity; individuality; and the claims, or lack of claims, of time and mundane purpose that

3. *Dictionary of American Biography*, 22:473.

were hard to come by in the society that was growing up around New Hampshire. And it may be that what was true, for artists and philosophers, was, in ways unstated or unrecognized, true also for those worldly summer people, the boarders, in July and August—the men and women in cottages wedged in along the shores of ponds, and all who came for shorter visits to climb, to camp, and just to look. One would like to think so.

Whatever happened to all those people in their total numbers—and each year the number grew by the thousands— they did something for and to the state. In their totality, for one thing, they became a business. By the turn of the century, the cash received from summer people was estimated at about $700,000 each season. A few years later, the amount of money invested in summer hotels, boarding houses, and lake cottages alone was believed to be about $50 million. By any economic measurement, this was all to the good; the activity contributed substantially to the welfare of the state.

What it all meant sociologically is, and always will be, a matter for debate. On the one hand, there are the presumed advantages—wider horizons, for instance—to be obtained by exposure to ways of life and purposes other than one's own. On the other hand, there are the attitudes developed when one serves the desires of others, especially of others who do not at the time seem to be doing very much and who can afford to do what they want. In any event, the state became in these days a society used by others—exploited by those who came into it from other places. Whether they came to write books, or paint pictures, or create statues, or invite the soul, or gambol in the shadow of a mountain, or see each other at the Kearsarge House, or to finance the making of cotton cloth by others, or to build a railroad—no matter why they came, they arrived at times of their own choosing, seeking their own conditions, and in pursuit of their own special interests. This got worse before it got better.

15

A Second Chance

*T*HE benign invasions of the idle, the rich, and the talented; the ceaseless clacking of machinery along the Merrimack; the boisterous labor in the North Country in the years between the Civil War and World War I—none of these could conceal the fact that New Hampshire was a society on the way down. In each succeeding decade, it lost ground in real wealth and in population within the expanding nation. In its political exercises, it reflected the somber fact that in its own life nothing much was really happening. These exercises were conducted, on the whole, by Republicans. From 1864 to 1914, there were twenty-five governors of whom two were Democrats. The Grand Old Party did not bring to the management of affairs, for most of these years, either the sense of purpose or the quality of excitement that had marked the Democrats in the first half of the century. The most generous-minded chronicler of the state's history was forced in retrospect to admit that while, without exception, the "governors were men of sincerity and ability, yet it is hard to distinguish one from another after the lapse of the years." [1] It was hard even at the time and, as with the governors so with most of the others who held office.

The exception strikingly proving the rule, however, was William E. Chandler. One of the most powerful men in the politics

1. Squires, *The Granite State*, 1:413.

of the state during this period, he was also by far the most interesting—indeed one of the most interesting in the whole country.
Owner of the Concord *Monitor and Statesman*, he served in the
administrations of Lincoln and Johnson. As a member of the national committee of the Republican party, he had played a principal part—indeed some said the dominating role—in devising
the tactics that wrenched the presidency from Samuel Tilden in
the disputed election of 1876. In later years, he was secretary of
the navy when the first keels were laid down for what later became known as the "Great White Fleet." And after that, from
1887 to 1901, he was a persistent if erratic force in national politics as senator from New Hampshire.

The foundations for this career were laid as far back as 1865,
when Chandler, like many of his fellows, left the state because
it was apparent to him "that the progress of any young lawyer
in Concord was limited by the size of the community." [2] Settling in Washington, he represented the interests of the Union
Pacific Railroad, the Western Union Telegraph Company, the
National Life Insurance Company, and the various concerns of
Jay Cooke. Like many others who in this time went forth to exercise their brains and skills in other places, he left his heart in
New Hampshire. And, also like them, he retained, as a locus
for his affections, a piece of ground, a summer home in the
state. In his case, the large "unsightly," commodious house in
Warner, with its great views to the west and north, served to
justify and validate his powerful influence in the political life of
the state he had, to all intents and purposes, left.

In one very significant area of that political life, Chandler
made himself especially felt. Beneath the surface, where from
one year to the next one governor looked like another and every
party platform was built from the planking of the last election,
there was not so much an exciting issue as a determining current
that flowed—often silently—through all the state's affairs. The
energy in this current was the railroad. It will be remembered
that the Democrats in the earlier years, fearing business and mo-

2. Richardson, *William E. Chandler*, p. 51.

nopoly, had contrived legislation to divide transport services
into small sections. As it happened, the thing had been over-
done. By 1870, a thousand miles of track were cut up among
thirty-two separate companies. One road had three miles of
right-of-way; another, four and three-quarters, and a third, five
and a quarter. Slowly the claims of economic good sense began
to make headway; in the years after the Civil War, consolidation
of these resources through purchase or lease was increasingly
achieved. The move toward combination was considerably accelerated by the bankruptcy of many of the smaller companies.
One of the products of this concentration of assets was the Concord road which ran down the Merrimack River and totally controlled the traffic in Manchester. Only 141 miles long it was,
nevertheless, an agency of great power. The lines and rolling
stock were carefully maintained, the service was reliable, the
stations in Concord and Merrimack were appropriately imposing
monuments, and dividends were a steady 10 per cent.

Off in the south east corner of the state there were thirty-five
miles of track that formed a section of the main line from Boston to Portland. This was the property of the Boston and Maine
Railroad, a corporation in the Commonwealth of Massachusetts.
By 1883, these two companies—the Concord and the Boston
and Maine—had so far proceeded with their consolidation programs that they had become the dominant carriers in the state.
In that year they put forward a scheme to further extend their
holdings. The Boston and Maine would take over the Eastern,
thus acquiring control over all traffic in the south and east,
while the Concord would acquire the Northern and the Boston,
Concord, and Montreal which would give it control over all the
traffic in the upper part of the state. This proposal was made
public thirty days before the new legislature—already elected—
was to meet. It was at that point that William Chandler went to
work.

He had, for some time, foreseen that the railroads—with their
consolidating power obtained by purchase or lease—would
present a threat to the political life of the state and would, more
especially, threaten to place the Republican party in "degrading

subjection to railroad control and direction." [3] In 1881, therefore, he had been instrumental in preventing a merger of the
Concord with the Boston and Lowell. Two years later, presented with the scheme of the Concord and the Boston and
Maine, he mounted his opposing argument in the pages of his
paper, the Concord *Monitor and Statesman*. He understood, he
said, the economic advantages of combination, but was appalled
by this sudden effort to alter the ancient principle of competition
that had, from the beginning, served as the foundation of state
railroad policy. He was especially annoyed that the planned
combinations would be put before a legislature that had been
elected by citizens who had not had a chance to consider the
issue for themselves. Then he said:

> These two corporations will rule New Hampshire with a rod of
> iron. They will debauch and control both political parties, subsidize
> and destroy every newspaper, retain every lawyer, nominate every
> legislator and fill his pockets with free passes or mileage books,
> select the presiding officers of both Houses; name the Committees
> and secure the legislative action or non-action needed. Whenever
> they wish any new privilege they will not ask it from the legislature,
> but will usurp and defiantly exercise it and rely on the dilatoriness
> and evasiveness of the Courts, the organization and appointment of
> the Judges of which they will control through their subsidized legis-
> latures and Governors. [4]

In that short paragraph much—most—of the essential political history of the state for the next twenty years was set forth.
Chandler, by his reiterated effort, could slow the tide he had
predicted but he could not contain it. For one thing, when he
wrote these words he was Secretary of the Navy in Washington,
forced to press his points home to party leaders from a distance.
For another thing he was ahead of his time. The immediate need
in New Hampshire, as in other states, was to introduce stability
to the disorderly system that had been built up in the first days
of the railroad fever. To achieve a sensible transport organization, it was necessary to eliminate some meaningless short lines;
to consolidate the resources of competing services; to wring the

3. Richardson, *William E. Chandler*, p. 278.
4. Richardson, *William E. Chandler*, p. 361.

water out of unrealistic stock issues; to strengthen structures of management—in a word, to find economies of proper scale. All the forces of survival were concentrated on the effort to drive out the ancient faith in competition among small parts. Against these forces, Chandler and his followers could exert a modifying influence but could not prevail.

During the years that followed, the power of the railroads in New Hampshire increased steadily, and among the railroads, the authority of the Boston and Maine moved, equally steadily, toward ascendancy. By 1895, that railroad—better-financed, more skillfully managed, far larger since it had rights-of-way in four states—controlled almost all the trackage in the state. In the opinion of the most thorough and careful student of these matters, "it was not too much to say . . . New Hampshire was governed by a dictatorship, with the railroad in the position of dictator." [5]

The means by which this absolute rule was achieved were similar to the methods used by other roads in other states. They have been fully described by others in many outraged or sorrowing pages, but a word or two here will not be redundant. The foundation of the sovereignty established by the Boston and Maine was the free pass and the retainer. The free pass was given to various deserving or prominent citizens, but more especially to men in public life—particularly to those serving in public office and invariably to those in the legislature. The retainer was offered to all rising young lawyers. That most of these attorneys accepted appointments and attendant fees is suggested by the fact that people with claims against the Boston and Maine often had great difficulty finding someone to plead their case because so many in the legal profession were serving as counsel to the railroad.

Using such levers, it was not difficult to infiltrate the internal workings of the government, which was not designed to work particularly well anyway.

Immediately beneath the governor was the council, an agency designed by the founders (who had had a lively recollection of

5. Richardson, *William E. Chandler*, p. 623.

George III) to constrain an unruly governor. This agency of five members had the power to reject any appointments made by the chief magistrate. Its members were elected from five large districts by citizens who often did not know the candidates, and even more often did not know or care much about the presumed duties of the council. Throughout its history, the council has proved to be more of a nuisance than an imaginative instrument of government, but in the 1880s and 1890s, with its power over appointments, it was an instrument admirably designed to protect the interests of the Boston and Maine.

In the legislature, there was the Senate—twenty-four men somewhat removed from the individual voters by the size of their districts, and the House—described at various times as the largest, second largest, or third largest deliberative body in the world. In 1880, it had more than 400 members. They were obviously more immediately responsive to the will of the people than were senators or councilmen—some of them represented fewer than 100 constituents. Since, on the whole, these legislators were sensitive primarily to their own local interest, and since the turnover in each session was considerable, the leadership in the House tended to fall on a few seasoned veterans who received careful attention from the legal counsel and special agents of the railroad. Finally, there was the railroad commission, whose chairman, Henry Putney, held the office from 1886 to 1909. During that extended period, public opinion held that no step was ever taken by the commission to which the railroads could reasonably have the shadow of an objection.

The system as thus designed and nourished worked for almost thirty years in the best interests of the Boston and Maine Railroad. Since it got about what it wanted with a minimum of effort, it acted as a benevolent and satisfied despot. Indeed, it appears, that for much of this period almost everyone was satisfied with the arrangement. The railroad was a public service, an obvious asset, a self-evident necessity. To serve it in small ways for small returns was in the nature of things. It was normal for lawyers to have retainers against the possibility of rendering advice and counsel in the future; it was not out of the way for legislators who had to make their way to the capital by railroad to receive recognition of their official positions—a respectful gesture toward their eminence—in the form of a pass. And for the men in the railroad, and especially for Lucius Tuttle, the president in his Boston office, the state of affairs was also in the nature of things. How else could one seek to manage effectively an expanding and extending enterprise, whose workings were directly attended with public consequences and therefore sensitive to public attitudes? In a strange way, this situation seems to have satisfied most people most of the time. As the editor of the *Granite State Press* said, "the Boston and Maine has given the State a *good* government and has always been regardful of the interests of the Republican Party." [6]

Through all the years after 1883, Chandler, however, remained unsatisfied and continued his attack on what came to be called the Great Corporation. In 1901, after twelve years in the U.S. Senate, Chandler was defeated for re-election. His opponent was Henry Burnham, a "polished and colorless personality" who faithfully represented railroad attitudes. At the start of the campaign, the company sought to "cut Mr. Chandler's throat with a feather" by proclaiming its neutrality in the forthcoming election. But since the senator remained undamaged by such a fragile weapon, the plan had to be changed. Chandler described the situation in a letter which his biographer said contained the essential truth:

> Railroad consultation was held and it was decided that it was necessary to throw off the mask [of neutrality] and rally the railroad forces and this was done. Every pass holder was sent for; the railroad headquarters became the headquarters of Mr. Burnham. You know the methods. Open railroad appeals, free passes innumerable, money without stint was expended and within forty-eight hours my forces were reduced or broken. [7]

By such means the Boston and Maine Railroad brought their great adversary down and elevated in his stead a man who never raised his voice in the Senate chamber and always voted "right."

6. Richardson, *William E. Chandler*, p. 625.
7. Richardson, *William E. Chandler*, p. 638.

But Chandler left behind him a considerable legacy. Earlier than almost anyone in the whole country (he liked to think of himself as the first Progressive), he had discerned the dangers that might attend the astonishing development of rail transport. In countless speeches, numberless editorials, and in a remarkable pamphlet called *New Hampshire: A Slave State,* he had sought to describe how a rich and powerful corporation could capture the direction of both political parties. He had also set forth the methods by which the energy in this novel industrial force could be contained and directed to useful purposes. In so doing, he prepared both an informed constituency and a program for those who came after him.

Those who did come after appeared from unexpected places in the structure of New Hampshire politics. The first broke the mold from which so many of the preceding governors had been cast. He was John McLane, born in Scotland, trained as a cabinet maker, proprietor of a furniture factory in Milford. During his service in the House and Senate at the state capital in Concord, he had demonstrated an awareness of what was going on around him and a willingness to entertain thoughts of change. He remained a good friend of William Chandler in spite of all the party differences with that restless man, and was one of the many men in public life at the turn of the century whose liberal spirit and enlightened intentions were reinforced and given focus by Theodore Roosevelt. In 1904, the great Roosevelt election year, McLane became governor of the state by a large majority. As governor, he took an active part in the arrangements leading up to the Portsmouth Peace Conference in 1905; acted to block the construction of a race track designed not so much to improve the breed as to fill the pocketbooks of professional gamblers; and began a modest program for the conservation of forests. More significantly, he suggested by his presence that there was a place in the party for those of his liberal persuasion.

What followed was an altogether surprising break from the past. Sometime around the turn of the century, a man named Winston Churchill came to Cornish to settle among the artists. He had been born in St. Louis, educated at the United States Naval Academy, and had then decided to try his hand at writing novels. He was an entertaining man, without pretention, a shrewd observer of men at work. There was a streak of mysticism in him and a relaxed independence from conventional constraints that sometimes took interesting forms. A quite correct cousin from Missouri was once appalled when she went to call on him in Cornish to find him grinning down at her from a tree—stark naked.

Such assets of training, temperament, and talent are not, ordinarily, of the kind to turn a man's mind to matters political, nor of the kind to send a man rapidly up the ladder of politics at any time—and especially of the politics of New Hampshire at that time. Winston Churchill seems, in fact, to have sought public office at first simply as a way of getting material for one of his works of fiction. His first novels had dealt with the history of this country—the Revolution, the Civil War, the settling of Kentucky. It occurred to him that, if he could be of some service to the state, he might learn things that would enable him to write more intelligently about the contemporary scene. Accordingly, he stood for the legislature as a representative from Cornish and was elected. In two terms, he discovered that his fellow legislators liked him, and he also found out a great deal about how the state was run. He began to write a book called *Coniston,* which was based on the career of Ruel Durkee and which explained the workings of a political machine in detail. It was published in 1906.

In that same year, thirteen citizens of the state wrote Churchill a letter asking if he would run for governor. Seven of these men were lawyers, two were editors of small-town papers, two were businessmen, one was a professor, and one was a physician. Only two of them had had any previous experience—in both cases brief—in public life. Their object was to find somebody who could carry the fight to the railroads. Churchill, during his terms in the legislature, had come to understand the nature of the great corporation (he later wrote a novel describing how a railroad could dominate a state) and accepted the invitation. Then he and his backers turned to William Chandler.

Together they framed a nine-point program. The first five points dealt with the railroads—elimination of passes; election of railroad commissions by the people; accurate evaluation of railroad property; a corrupt-practices act and publicity for campaign contributions; registration of lobbyists and publication of their retainers. The program also proposed the creation of a tax commission and passage of a primary election law.

Armed with this program and a candidate, the handful of men calling themselves the Lincoln Republican Club set out to win the nomination for Churchill at the party convention in September. The odds against them were staggering. Save for Chandler all involved at first were without much experience or any influence within the party; the effort had begun at the last hour—a little more than two months before the convention; the candidate was a new man in the state and a poor speaker. Chandler himself warned that it was a two-campaign war; no one who could not take defeat calmly in 1906 to fight again in 1908 should consider enlisting in the venture.

The amazing thing is that they almost won the election. Churchill went up and down the state convincing people, in his unassuming way, of his dedication to the task of defeating the corporation and the corporation's political machine. As the weeks passed, increasing numbers gathered in the ranks. Then, in a wild and unruly convention, Churchill, on the eighth ballot, established a lead over his three most obvious opponents. This so frightened the party leaders that they quickly united behind the least competent candidate and, on the ninth ballot, pushed him past Churchill and, in November, into the governor's chair.

The following year, the Lincoln Republican Club—as often happens in such cases—disintegrated because of friction produced by varying aims and differing personalities. But, as does not often happen in such cases, it left behind solid, compelling consequences. As a result of this campaign, there was a leaven of reformers in the legislature, a defined program for these new men to concentrate upon, and—most of all—the demonstration of a powerful spirit at work within the state. During the next four years, the legislature passed a series of enlightened laws restricting, if not abolishing, the use of the free railroad pass; instituting a study that later produced the desired tax commission;

and establishing a direct primary system to nominate candidates for public office.

Serving within the legislature in these years—two terms in the House and one term in the Senate—was a man named Robert P. Bass. He had been a leader in the movement for the new legislation and had, as a result, acquired both a following and considerable political skill. In 1910, he announced himself as a Republican candidate for governor. Like Winston Churchill, Bass was something of a sport in the political lineage of the state. He was young (thirty-six), originally from the Middle West, and a poor speaker. But he knew the state far better than did his friend from Cornish and he was better known. After finishing Harvard College and studying at the Harvard Law School, he had spent most of his time at the home of his ancestors in Peterborough. There he had managed a large dairy farm and devoted much of his time to the development of sensible methods of forestry in the state. Bass was one of those young men who had been profoundly influenced, first by Gifford Pinchot and then by Theodore Roosevelt. As a result, he became a convinced conservationist and that interest led him into state politics. Added to these qualifications of experience and concern was the fact that he had a good deal of money.

Offsetting these advantages were the timeless objections. He had too much money; he came from Chicago; he was putting himself forward ahead of the deserving (those who had for so long worked to tighten the bolts that held the machine together); he said right out loud hard things about conditions in the state simply to advance his own career—and so on and so on. So great was the feeling against him among party members that Chandler reached the conclusion that Bass could not possibly be elected. Only when the search for a reasonable substitute failed did the old man reluctantly come round. Once committed, however, he threw himself with his customary forthright passion into the Bass cause.

During the spring and summer of 1910, Bass increasingly demonstrated that he was quite capable of supporting that cause himself. He travelled continuously around the state—speaking morning, noon, and night to anyone who would listen. There was little style in his manner and less art in his delivery, but despite his halting words, he came through as an absolutely honest man who understood the troubles of the state and was prepared to describe exactly what he would do about them. And he had one great line that has entered the political folklore of New Hampshire. It dealt with what became the principal point of attack against him—that as a rich man, not one of us, he was simply trying to buy the governorship. He was indeed spending money to get elected, he said over and over again—and then, in the memory of one of his campaign managers and many others, he would clench his right fist and cry out: "But whose money is it? It is my money and not the money of the Boston and Maine Railroad." [8] He then promised to make public all the receipts and expenditures of his campaign.

Beneath the words and promises and money and impressions there was a further asset. Bass was quite willing to spend a good deal of time and hard work cultivating the grass roots. No city ward was considered too firmly in the hands of the Old Guard, no town believed too small to escape attention. Throughout the state, he sought and found chairmen and workers devoted to him and to the cause. In September it all paid off. In the first primary election to select candidates for governor ever held in the state, Bass won a spectacular victory, piling up almost twice the vote of his nearest rival. And in November, in a year of Democratic success across the nation, he beat his opponent by a considerably larger margin than Republican candidates had received in the three preceding elections. Just as gratifying, and more important for the future of the state, the election filled the legislature with like-minded men.

There was thus a coalition of power at the center of the state government which could shape the future for some time to come. The acts of the legislature which met in 1911, when Robert Bass assumed the governorship included: the creation of a public service commission, one of the first in the nation, with

8. William Caldwell to one of the authors in 1928. The phrase, in various minor changes of form, appears in many accounts, contemporary and historical, of the campaign.

power to regulate corporate organization, rate structures, and operating procedures in all agencies rendering public services in communication, utilities, and transport; the requirement to make public all campaign contributions and expenditures; a pure food law; a factory inspection law; a new and more extensive law controlling child labor; a law creating a state tax commission to set fair evaluations and assessments for corporations; a workmen's compensation law; a law extending the areas and strengthening the administration of forestry reserves. The governor failed to persuade the legislature to accept the proposed amendment to the Constitution permitting a federal income tax, but in almost all other cases the executive and legislative branches of the state government saw eye to eye.

Between 1910 and 1912, New Hampshire achieved a place in the national consciousness that it had not held since the great days of Jacksonian Democracy. And, as on that previous occasion, its claim to attention was that it represented attitudes that were somewhat ahead of the times. The state had assumed, in Theodore Roosevelt's words, a radical position. In the matter of controlling private corporations, regulating public utilities, and protecting the interests of men and women working within the industrial process, New Hampshire in two years more nearly fulfilled the stated and promised objectives than any other state in the Union, with the probable exception of Wisconsin. And what in 1910 seemed radical in New Hampshire became, in not so many years, commonplace throughout the nation.

The remarkable accomplishments of this period had been a long time in the making and were the product of many men and varied influences. One can start back in 1883, when Chandler claimed that the "grand consolidation of all the state's railroads" would transfer control to "capitalists of Massachusetts, without any opportunity for the people of the state to be heard from." [9] As he pounded out his points down through the years, he was not rewarded by much positive action, but he prepared an increasingly larger audience for those who followed him. Among them, the most important probably were Winston

9. Richardson, *William E. Chandler*, p. 360.

Churchill—the first to mobilize the members of that audience into a ponderable voting influence—and Robert Bass, who expanded that influence into an organized majority. These two men, who came into the state from Missouri and Illinois, were helped immeasurably by forces outside the state—by a slowly emerging spirit of the times first given specific and local expression by such men as Robert La Follette in the Middle West and then, in the first decade of the new century, acquiring more generalized expression—and power—under the extraordinary leadership of Theodore Roosevelt. Under such sanctions, this emerging spirit became the nationwide Progressive movement—a supporting tide for the men in New Hampshire.

Those who came from the ranks of Chandler's audience to take active part in the development of the Progressive movement were, at first, like those who had written to invite Churchill to run for governor in 1906. They were, it will be recalled, owners of small businesses, editors of country papers, lawyers, doctors, professors, teachers—men who by virtue of special training or particular temperament had established themselves as independent and successful citizens. They were members, on the whole, of what is thought of today as the middle class. It was from such men that the Progressive movement originally derived its principal strength. They were less aware, by virtue of their experience, than many of their fellow citizens of the monotony, occasional danger, and dependent state created for workers in the lower reaches of industry. But, because of their independent positions, they were more sensitive to the possible meaning of continued unregulated corporate growth throughout the society. What Theodore Roosevelt called the wonderful new conditions of industrial development created an energy that, as Roosevelt said, could either destroy the society, shake it apart—or, properly controlled by the people, could be made to serve the people's interest. It was this sense of lurking dangers on the one hand and perceived opportunity on the other that excited the Progressives, and pulled them on toward Armageddon where they could battle for the Lord to the tune of "The Battle Hymn of the Republic."

In New Hampshire, the excitement was sufficient to produce

two years of great achievement. Then, as often happens, the culminating effort was followed by a divided purpose and fragmented energies. The seeds of such discord were in the ground from the beginning. Theodore Roosevelt wrote to William Allen White to explain how the Republican victory in 1910 had been achieved:

> You speak of New Hampshire as an ultra radical state where a clean, strong, uncompromising fight was made. I certainly should not advocate any fight being made unless it was clean and strong, but in New Hampshire we won because of just the kind of compromise to which I allude.[10]

The nature of that compromise was as follows. Because New Hampshire citizens wanted a decent, honest government in their own state and a voice in their own government, they elected a Progressive governor and liberal-minded state legislature in 1910. But because they really did not care much about what happened elsewhere—the tariff and the other things that Washington took care of—they voted to nominate two (Republican) stand-pat Congressmen. By this compromise, a precarious coalition of the liberal and conservative interests in the Republican party was achieved and by this coalition the election was won in a Democratic year.

In New Hampshire as in the nation, however, no spirit of compromise proved strong enough to hold the conflicting interests together for very long. In all the complicated and dangerous years that have followed 1910, the Republican party has possessed a riven spirit. There has been not so much a refreshing fusion of usefully opposing interests as an oscillation—the liberal influence intruding sporadically upon the commitment to keep things as they used to be while the world goes on changing. Yet, for a season, New Hampshire had recovered the sense that it could take care of itself and take charge of its future.

---

10. Theodore Roosevelt, *The Letters of Theodore Roosevelt*, edited by Elting E. Morison et al., 8 vols. (Cambridge, Mass.: Harvard University Press, 1951–1954), 3:184.

16

Another Opportunity

$\mathcal{A}$S with all wars, World War I was, for New Hampshire as for the other states, in one way a local and personal matter. Young men going off to fight and doing their part; mothers, fathers, wives, and sweethearts staying home and doing their part. Acts of bravery, endurance, anguish, sorrow, pride, and duty. All this takes place whether the fighting is at Bunker Hill, Chancellorsville, or in the Argonne Forest. In other ways, the war did not come home to the community in quite the way the earlier conflicts had made themselves felt. It was too brief, too far away, too abstract in stated purpose. Only later could it be seen that World War I had changed the future, closing out the nineteenth century and clearing the way for new times. The history of New Hampshire for the next fifty years was the history of a struggle to see whether what had been learned in the past and what was available in the way of present resources could be made to fit into the developing nature of those new, disorderly times.

The period opened in an ominous way. On February 2, 1922, the following notice was posted in all departments of the Amoskeag Manufacturing Company:

Commencing Monday February 13th a reduction of twenty percent will be made in all hours and piece rates in all Department of the Amoskeag. At the same time the running time of the mills will be

increased from 48 to 54 hours per week in accordance with the
schedule posted herewith. W. P. Straw, Agent.[1]

On February 10, in an election arranged by James Starr, vice-
president of the United Textile Workers, the employees of the
company, by a vote of 12,032 to 118, voted to reject the wage
cut and increase of working hours. On February 13, the walkout
started and the company closed down all the mills in a city that
lived by the work in the mills. Nine months and two weeks
later, the strike was settled essentially on the terms proposed in
Mr. Straw's first notice—with the added qualification that
leaders of the strike would not be rehired for their old positions.

When, after this extended period marked by the intransigence
of the owners, the orderliness of the strikers, and the stoic acceptance of the city, James Starr called off the strike, he said
that the main point had been achieved; the real issue had been
made explicit. This was the forty-eight-hour week, which could
only be obtained by legislation. To have made that point was
sufficient. In conclusion, he added: "The Amoskeag and Boston
and Maine have had a death grip on the state of New Hampshire
for the past fifty years. You have broken that grip." [2] Not
quite. At the next meeting of the legislature, a bill limiting the
work week to forty-eight hours was presented and defeated by a
combination of senators who represented manufacturing and
farming interests.

From the beginning of this long struggle, the argument of the
company had been that the Amoskeag could not withstand competition from the South, where men worked for half the wages
and for longer hours. Not many on the other side were convinced by this claim; it was argued that from 1911 to 1921 the
company had in fact made an average profit of $3 million a year
and the case, as stated in Boston, was not much strengthened
when, in the middle of the strike, the company declared a normal quarterly dividend of $1.50 a share.

At this remove, the strike at the Amoskeag, taken by itself,

1. William DeMoulpied, *History of the Amoskeag Strike* (Manchester, N.H.: Amoskeag Manufacturing Company, 1924), p. 1.
2. DeMoulpied, *Amoskeag Strike*, p. 177.

may be hard to fit into any sustaining context—like any antiquated period piece viewed from the presumed sophistication of contemporary times. There is the surprising discovery that no formal mechanism for the accommodation of differences existed, and the further recognition of a state of mind which accepted, in the absence of such mechanism, the cynical intransigence of absentee owners, on the one hand, and the patient endurance of workers on the other. But the significance of the strike lies not so much in its place in the history of labor relations as elsewhere. However arrogant in manner and self-serving in matter the position of the directors, as expressed through their instrument, Frederick Dumaine, may seem, those directors were responding to an actual condition.

The competition from the South, as ensuing events revealed ever more clearly, was real. Between 1880 and 1925, the number of spindles in New England doubled, while in the same years the number below the Mason and Dixon line increased thirtyfold. Three years after the strike there were, for the first time, more spindles in the South than in the North. In that year, also, the value of the southern product was considerably greater than that of the northerners. No dedication of labor, no simplification of method, no skill and imaginative acts of management—even had they been forthcoming—could alter the developing discrepancy between the rising and the fading powers.

The strike at the Amoskeag was simply an indication of that fact and a portent of things to come. For a decade, the fortunes of the company slid downhill in spite of a series of structural and financial manipulations, until its condition was referred to Arthur Black, as special master in bankruptcy. He declared that the kindest thing to do was to recommend that liquidation begin and that all the land, buildings, and equipment of the great company should be put up for public auction at once.

What seemed at first a total disaster for the city of Manchester turned in time into a small miracle. A group of citizens organized the Amoskeag Industries to buy (at a cost of $5 million) and to manage the huge property. In the next few years—in a remarkable display of energy, judgment, and forethought—this association found an infinite variety of small businesses to fill the great spaces and to employ more people than had, at the end, been on the payroll of the Amoskeag Manufacturing Company.

What had begun in Manchester as sudden, complete, dramatic catastrophe was in the following years translated through the state as a slowly spreading decline. A few statistics suggest the rate of decay within the textile industry. In 1935, there were still 1,095,000 cotton spindles in the state, but in that same year Hillsborough County—the principal source of production—lost 110,000 spindles. Fifteen years later, in 1950, one town in that county, which in the great days had had six working mills, contained only one small textile factory which concentrated on a special kind of fabric.

This is not to suggest that, as the years passed, the industry vanished completely from New Hampshire; in the census of 1970 textiles still held a place in the state's list of significant manufactures. But it is to indicate that the enterprise which had been the major prop and stay at the beginning of the century lost ground, both absolutely and in relation to other activities, as the century progressed.

Then there was that other prop and stay of former days—agriculture. For a long time, it will be recalled, the state had not been as much of a farming community as it liked to believe. But in 1910, at least a third of the working population, a somewhat greater number than those engaged in industry, still made their living on farms. Twenty years later the figure had been cut to 11.3 percent. This "very rapid shift" out of agriculture had created what a study commissioned by the Governor in 1936 called "a severe unbalance in the economy." Reflecting on this condition, the author of the study suggested that a continuation of the existing state might produce the end of private enterprise; indeed, he said, "Something in the nature of an involuntary socialization is actually happening." [3] And the social costs of this swift change were equally severe and apparent.

A different study of the 230 cities and towns in the state made in the same year reached the conclusion that 53 of the communi-

3. Samuel Crowther, *A Report to the Commission for the Promotion of the Wealth and Income of the People of New Hampshire* (Concord, N.H.: n.p., 1936), p. 25.

ties must be put in the category of "rural declining." Another
forty were called "rural-semi-recreational," of which thirty-two
could also be considered as "rural declining." In fact, to the
authors of this investigation, it appeared that at least 124
towns—or more than half the total—could be put on the borders
of the "rural declining" category. Only sixteen towns along the
principal river valleys, or in the lowlands near the city markets,
were discovered to derive their principal income from agriculture. And the contribution of agriculture to the state's total income in the year 1936 was reckoned to be 5.1 percent of the
whole.

These were the years—the retreat from the farm, the decline
of the textile industry, the Great Depression—during which people in many of the smaller towns seemed to live by taking in
each other's washing. They were also the years in which efforts
were made to deal systematically with developing problems
created by economic difficulties. The principal instrument was
the New Hampshire State Planning and Development Commission. Part of the task of this body was simply to keep statistics
on the current situation—available power sources, transport facilities, factory sites, population shifts, hotels, tourist facilities,
and so forth. The Commission—on the basis of those statistics
—advertised throughout the country the nature of the industrial
and recreational opportunities that existed throughout the state.
And its staff conducted research into the nature of new opportunities and negotiated with interested parties, both inside and
outside the state, for development of new kinds of enterprise.
The record suggests with what intelligence and skill these varied
tasks were conducted. In 1948, for instance, the Commission
reported that in the previous two years 167 new companies had
been established in 85 communities to make 49 different kinds
of products. They also reported the successful effort to create a
series of new recreational areas around the state and to increase
the number of summer homes—mostly for people from other
states—to over 20,000.

This 1948 report suggests the kind of activity that continued
over the next two decades. There was a steady flow of new industry into the state. Some of those new installations were

branches or divisions of large companies seeking to disperse their manufacturing processes, more were new, small, independent, precariously organized companies engaged in all sorts of light industry, much of it connected with the electrical trade. Among these, the mortality rate was considerable, but in most instances the new facilities that had been created were soon taken over by succeeding ventures and, as time passed, the state could lay claim to a considerable number of small, useful companies that had found a secure base for continued operation.

Supporting this industrial development was the expansion of recreational opportunities—more summer homes, more parks, better roads, more hotels, more ski lodges to attract the outdoor enthusiasts, the casual tourist, and the summer resident. Some feeling for the nature of this recreational development can be obtained from the following figures. In 1935, it was estimated that a million man days were spent in support of this activity, producing an income for the state of nearly $10 million. Thirty-five years later, in 1970, this second-largest industry contributed an estimated $300 million to the state.

How necessary—indeed, how indispensable—this money is to New Hampshire is not a matter for debate. In spite of all the intelligent effort that has gone into the development of industrial enterprise; in spite of the numerical success of this effort; in spite of the fact that, in terms of numbers employed out of the total working population, New Hampshire can be thought of as one of the highly industrialized states in the Union—in spite of all this, the economic base provided either by growing or making things remains as thin as a razor's edge. In the census of 1970, the annual value of farm products was less in only two states (West Virginia and Alaska), while, in the value of goods manufactured, New Hampshire ranked thirty-ninth. Of the eleven lower-ranking states, all save Alaska derived their principal income from agriculture. They were, in fact, farm states. Thus positioned near the statistical bottom, New Hampshire must cope with the very hard facts of American economic development. It is a fortunate thing that New Hampshire still retains those timeless assets and attractions—the lakes, the mountains, the forests, the white houses, brick churches, town commons—that appeal to those who currently seek the serenity and dignity of a previous time.

The politics of a society with such an economic base must be concerned, in the nature of things, more with the search for survival than with the construction of a brave new world. It is therefore exceedingly interesting that, at the beginning of this period, when the rest of the country was moving from the normalcy of Warren G. Harding to the steadiness of Calvin Coolidge, New Hampshire elected a governor who seemed to have the fire of the earlier Progressives in his eye. He was, in fact, the lineal descendant of Winston Churchill and Robert Bass. Like them, he was used to the life of the well-to-do; like them, he came originally from out-of-state (New York); like them, he was a poor speaker; and as with them, his sincerity burned through his struggle to make himself clear.

Somewhere along what would seem to many observers to be the easy path of his youth (a brownstone house on East 69th Street, St. Paul's School in Concord, New Hampshire, and Princeton University), John G. Winant developed a sobering concern for those who had to make their way over more rocky terrain. As a teacher at St. Paul's, he determined to do something to even out the chances and opportunities in the society. So he ran for the legislature from the seventh ward in Concord and was elected to the state legislature in 1916. He was one of 404 representatives, half of whom were over fifty years old and most of whom came from rural communities. In his first session, he introduced a bill to limit the labor of women and children to forty-eight hours a week, a minimum wage bill, a bill to establish a research bureau to aid in the drafting of new legislation, and a bill to abolish capital punishment. All these proposed pieces of legislation were defeated. As this legislative session ended, the country entered World War 1 and Winant, then twenty-eight years old, joined the army and went to France. There, to his surprise, he became the commander of an aircraft squadron, flying along the western front.

Upon his return, he re-entered New Hampshire politics—first as a state senator and then, in 1923, as a member of the House.

In the election of that year, Robert Bass returned to the legislature and for the next twelve months the two worked very closely together. Their immediate objective was the passage of the forty-eight-hour week, which the strike at the Amoskeag had thrust into the public consciousness. Joining them in their efforts was a young man named H. Styles Bridges, who started his long political career, surprisingly enough, as an aide to Robert Bass and as a progressive.

As it happened, they failed to achieve their immediate objective, but they had developed in that period a long-range legislative program and a political strategy. As a first step, Winant would run for governor in 1924, would probably be defeated in a campaign designed primarily to acquaint the electorate with the long-range program, and then, in 1926, he would run again for governor while Bass would be a candidate for the U.S. Senate.

In fact, Winant was elected in 1924 and laid before the legislature in his inaugural address thirty very specific proposals for the members to consider. Many of these had to do with ways to strengthen the fiscal and administrative procedures in the government, and with new means to encourage the state's economic growth. Most of these carefully thought through, clearly stated proposals were passed into law. But the governor failed to achieve three of his primary objectives—the passage of the forty-eight hour bill, the ratification of a child labor amendment to the state constitution, and the passage of a more generous workmen's compensation bill.

In his two years in office, Winant made a considerable personal impression on the citizens but not enough to carry him to victory in 1926. He was defeated in the Republican primary, as was Robert Bass—who ran for the party's nomination for the U.S. Senate against George Moses. In this primary election Bass, who had for so long been the managing intelligence among the progressive members of the party, stood for public office for the last time. In the years that followed, he exerted such influence as he could—both in Concord and Washington—by using the weight of his experience, reputation, political wisdom, and, as some insisted, money, in support of the liberal impulses in the Republican party. For John Winant there remained quite a different future.

In 1930, he ran again for governor and was elected, in a Democratic year, by an impressive majority. And in the next election in 1932, the year of Franklin D. Roosevelt, he won again—running far ahead of anyone in the Republican party. What occurred in those four years was in many ways a personal triumph. At the beginning, Governor Winant carried the legislature along on such favorite projects of his as finding ways to increase the administrative efficiency of the state government and to extend the range of state support to small businesses and to the unemployed or unemployable. As the depression deepened, he moved steadily away from the ancient faiths of his party toward the precepts of the developing New Deal. Working with increasing ease among Democrats, both in Concord and Washington, he obtained legislation, administrative assistance, and money to cushion the shocks of the economic disaster of the 1930s. From the Civilian Conservation Corps and the National Planning Board he received impressive support for all kinds of projects that gave work to New Hampshire's unemployed and, where necessary, he found ways to supply both food and lodging for those on relief.

It was not only what he did, but the way he did it. For one thing, he appeared to work twenty-four hours a day; for another thing, he seemed ready to see anyone—his door was open to everyone—and, since everyone could not come to Concord, he travelled ceaselessly to inspect, to report, and to talk. What came through his indefatigable—almost feverish—commitment to the task was a sense of selflessness which in that time was, no doubt, more useful than any specific program. Some people began to speak of him as a president in 1936 and others were put in mind of Lincoln. Inevitably, his time and energy were spent in shoring up in New Hampshire an economy that was coming apart everywhere in the nation. He was, in other words, engaged in a holding operation. It would be interesting to know what he would or could have done had he been permitted to introduce those purposes he had developed in the 1920s into the life of the state in more normal, less desperate times than the 1930s.

As things turned out, it was a good many years before the state came back to times that anyone could think of as normal. During the 1930s there was persistent economic maladjustment, which was followed in the 1940s by the profound dislocations of World War II. And then, in what seemed at first to be the peace, there was a continuation of the pervasive unsettled condition that afflicted the whole country. During this period, the situation in the state was further complicated by the slow and steady erosion of the old primary industries—textiles, shoes, hosiery, and paper. And, as another telltale symptom, though the population was still slowly growing, it was also growing older. In 1952, the proportion of citizens over sixty-five to the rest of the citizens was greater in New Hampshire than in any other state in the Union. If many complained, at this time and later, that the members of the legislature were as old as grandfathers, it could at least be said that they fairly represented many of their constituents.

The problem, given all these forbidding conditions, was what the state could do with and for itself. Successive governors and legislators pursued the obvious, promising to do what they could to promote efficiency in government, to attract new industry, and to expand the tourist trade. But in the continuing straitened circumstances, a mood of monetary and philosophical caution concerning the appropriate sphere of state government not surprisingly developed: frugal budgets, limited action, minimum taxes on the individual. One administration after another rode into office with the commitment to avoid a broad-based tax—such as a sales tax or a tax on earned income.

Such attitudes, historically, have been associated primarily with the Republican party, and most New Hampshire administrations after World War II were Republican. As the Democrats in the period before the Civil War had acted in the faith of Thomas Jefferson, and the Progressives in the first decades of this century had acted in the faith of Theodore Roosevelt, so the Republicans, it often seemed, clung to the essential convictions of William McKinley. The mood, it also seemed, fitted the desires of most members of the society and was continuously celebrated in an interesting combination of assertion and invective by the *Manchester Union Leader*, a newspaper believed by many to be the most powerful institutional influence in New Hampshire politics since the disintegration of the Boston and Maine Railroad. What this paper stands for—and, more particularly, against—is clearer than what power it actually has over the citizenry. A recent study concludes, "Whether or not the *Union Leader* influence on the electorate is real, New Hampshire politicians perceive the connection as valid." [4]

There was, of course, a price to pay. Because there was not much money, there was not much the state could do. It still contributes, for instance, less per student and per capita to its institutions of higher learning than any other state in the Union. But it got by. For one thing, the federal government made available to New Hampshire, as it does to all states, funds for a variety of purposes. For another thing, while avoiding broad-based taxes on the citizens, the state had recourse to other kinds of levies— on liquor, tobacco, and horse racing. At times, the cash from these sources made up about two-thirds of the state's income from all taxes. And when these revenues were discovered to need further supplement, the state began, in 1964, to run the first legal sweepstakes lottery that had been conducted in the country in seventy-five years. The principle purpose of this exercise was to relieve the burden on the towns that were steadily having to increase their property taxes to support the local schools.

By these devices, the state kept itself going into the decade of the 1960s, retaining a precarious position in the national consciousness as a vacationland, a place to retire to, and as the state where, every four years, the first presidential primaries are held. This last, an almost pointless, rather harmless form of self-inflicted exploitation by outside elements, became in time a cause for general public notice and some local excitement. So, on the whole it was a period of getting by and, it seemed, of putting in time—some of it time borrowed from the past.

4. Eric Veblen, *The Manchester Union Leader in New Hampshire Elections* (Hanover, N.H.: The University Press of New England, 1975), p. 174.

And then, quite suddenly, everything—or almost everything—changed. The census of 1970 revealed that the population of New Hampshire, which had been 606,921 in 1960, had grown to 737,681. That was a jump of twenty-one percent—twice the rate of the national increase. For the first time since the census was taken in 1790, the state had grown more rapidly than the country as a whole. Beyond that, by a projection made in 1974, New Hampshire is expected to double its number in the next twenty-five years. By the year 2000, it may hold about 1.5 million people. This, indeed, was a whole new ball game.

The causes are many and varied. To name a few, there is, first of all, the highway program proposed for the whole country by Dwight D. Eisenhower when he was president. With its share of highway funds, New Hampshire has built a system of roads that makes it an easy state to get around in and into and out of—at least from North to South. This has opened up the state to members, in growing number, of the affluent society of the 1960s and early 1970s—the old who wish to retire to a place fairly close to bigger cities; the young who wish to get away from the technological jungles they grew up in, to construct new lives for themselves in simpler surroundings; the middle-aged who hope to escape surburbia, who are attracted by the favorable personal tax structure, and who are prepared to commute to work in other states. Taking these groups all together, they include a good many people.

Then there is the "second home society"—those people who divide their time between a place in Massachusetts, Rhode Island, or Connecticut, and a place in New Hampshire. In New Hampshire, they may have an isolated, renovated farm-house or, with growing frequency, they may live in a condominium development where they have several acres of their own, a screen of pine and spruce, a handsome modern house—and access to a social center, a ski run, a pond or swimming pool or both, a network of trails for riding or walking. All these advantages are obtained without the need to worry about plowing snow, the availability of plumbers, or police protection. The condominium, until now, has been one of the principal instruments in land development.

Then there is industry. What in earlier days had been an energy dedicated to the mass production of simpler things—rubber, steel, automobiles—that could be made more easily in other places than New Hampshire—has evolved into all the varied sophistications of the new technology. There is a need for small and refined parts—ball bearings, automatic controls, neat castings, fine wires, intricate circuits, and so forth. Working conditions, efficiency of transport, scale of operation, proximity to the intellectual institutions technology lives by—all conspire to make New Hampshire an excellent place to make such things. What began, after World War II, along Route 128 in Massachusetts spread steadily across the borders into the neighboring state. For the first time in many years, New Hampshire is now developing in its southern regions a solidly founded, rapidly developing industrial base of its own.

Then there are those who have come to serve the needs of all the others—the doctors, lawyers, merchants, restaurateurs, builders, developers, mechanics, stereo dealers. Some of them minister not so much to the bodily, practical, mundane needs that everybody develops in the course of the day's work: in growing number, there are men and women who are trying to construct a fresh and interesting setting for the life of the community. They start new magazines, run theaters, own galleries, organize musical groups, and seek in all possible ways to make available the kinds of intellectual stimulation that is supposed to survive only in big cities. One center for such activities lies along the Connecticut River valley; it derives much of its initial strength, as such activities invariably do, from an institution of higher learning, Dartmouth College in Hanover. Another is in the southeast and has as its source of stimulation the State University at Durham.

There is, thus, in terms of numbers, variety of endeavors, levels of training and ability, and available human energy, more going on in the state than ever before in its history. But as always where there is rising opportunity, there are obvious problems. For one thing there is the primordial geography of the state, which from the beginning set the conditions for its development into several different kinds of communities. Geography is a controlling factor. The North Country has not yet been much touched by the new stimulation, because much of the new growth is concentrated along the southern border—especially in a band about thirty miles wide running from Nashua to Keene.

These geographical divisions are accentuated by conflicting interests in the growing population. Some have come seeking to live a modern life amid the last enchantments of the nineteenth century and wish to keep the greens and commons and white houses and lovely villages exactly as they were. Some want to make things as efficiently as possible, using the modern means of production without much interest in their effect on the surroundings. Some want to create new kinds of communities, separate from the existing scheme, making use of the ancient ways of doing things. Some, having lived here all their lives, are ready to stand pat, taking such advantage from the new energies swirling around them as may come their way. Some want to make a fortune by investing in the construction of everything from cheap mass housing projects to elaborate artificial communities where members do everything but work—as at Hilton Head, South Carolina.

One way or another, all these diverse groups confront what has become the first order of business in the state today—land use. It is presented in many forms. For instance, the town of Amherst—beyond all doubt one of the most charming villages in New Hampshire—had a population of 1,622 in 1820; 1,353 in 1870; about 1,500 in 1950; and in 1970, after another twenty years of growth, about 7,000 people lived there. Not far from Amherst lies Milford where, in 1950, a piece of the last farmland in the area was sold to a new company for $150 an acre. That land is now worth $10,000 an acre.

It is not all a matter of numbers and dollars. What is the meaning in terms of jobs, pollution, taxes, and social change, of siting a pulp mill or a nuclear energy plant or an oil refinery in this or that section of the state? What is the cost, aesthetically, of the long rows of tacky one-story establishments and blinking neon lights that seem inevitably to grow on the fringes of an industrial strip? How long will it take those who came to New Hampshire to get out of suburbia to build new suburbias along the throughways?

These are the kinds of questions that have been raised because, in the decade from 1960 to 1970, the conditions of modern times—of the twenty-first century—flooded over the borders and into the state. The tendency, not surprisingly, had been to deal with these questions, when they are raised as details, by default: Let these small, cheap, clapboard developments get built, it will be good for the town; let these neon signs, secondhand car lots, and pizza parlors extend along the highway, it will be good for trade. There is something to be said for this way of doing things; it is the way many of the gristmills, sawmills, and small textile mills came into the communities in the old days.

When the question seems much bigger than a detail, something that, all at once, appears a clear and present distortion in the community—a big housing development in a pleasant valley, a refinery along the coast, an east-west highway through developing industrial areas—the tendency has been to organize groups and stop it. There is something also to be said for this way of doing things. From the beginning, citizens aroused about great issues—such as the building of barracks for British troops by New Hampshire men in Boston and abolition—have taken useful action.

But in the present instance it does not seem that either benign neglect or sporadic resistance to one proposal or another will serve. What is happening in New Hampshire, as elsewhere in the country, is the development of a thing called the technological society. That society rests on an elaborate system designed to make and deliver all kinds of goods and services to its members. So sophisticated is that system—and so powerful—that it is now able to build an environment for our lives that can, in effect, take the place of the natural setting.

As in any system, what happens in one part of it in time affects all the other parts. If, for instance, people in this technological environment want to use electricity to heat their houses, cook their meals, light their rooms, cool their bodies, and keep the television on six hours a day, somewhere sources for the energy needed to produce this power—oil refineries, hydroelectric plants, or nuclear stations—must be constructed, even if those same people don't like the way such installations look or the way they clog the atmosphere. If people want the public benefits of health care, education, or social security in its largest sense, they must accept the necessity for the industrial development from which this century makes its living, and recognize the need for a tax structure that will support the desired benefits. If they value the gracious ways of living suggested by greens and commons and woods and scenery, as well as communities built to the scale of the local and the personal, they must figure out suitable locations, conditions, and controls for housing the indispensable industries—and the people who work in the new factories—on which the general welfare of the society depends.

The choice before the residents of New Hampshire, as for all residents in the country, no longer seems to include the possibility of preserving, as if in amber, some small, attractive corner of the past. The rate of general change is too great and too pervasive.

In this situation, the future prospects for everyone are self-evidently precarious. There is the school of thought that holds that the forces of technology are using up all the available materials so fast that soon there will be nowhere to go but down. There is the school that holds that these forces in the system are probably perpetual and certainly irreversible, and that in time the machines will do us all in. Even for those who do not quite believe our world is going to fall or fly apart, it is obvious that we are going to have a very hard time putting the pieces together in a new and satisfying way.

It is odd to discover that, in times of such general peril, the future of New Hampshire may well be more in its own hands than it has been for 150 years. The state has more human energy, more varieties of competence, more sources of economic vitality, more sense of the need to think of future possibilities than ever before in its history. Besides, it is small; whatever decisions are agreed upon can be quickly transmitted through the whole. Furthermore, the undirected course of its technological development has not yet proceeded to the point where it is beyond sensible modification and control.

How, given these conditions, can the state proceed? There are some precedents that it may be useful to have in mind in seeking to deal with those forces of technology that will provide the primary energy in shaping the future. In the 1840s, it was discovered that you cannot handle machinery by pretending it is not there, or by trying to legislate it out of existence. The locomotives and the big mills broke through the restraining clauses in the laws. In the 1880s and 1890s, it was discovered that if you left the machinery free to plot its own course it took over everything. The state's history became the history of the Amoskeag mills and the Boston and Maine Railroad. In the first decade of this century, it was discovered that while you could not keep the machinery of the modern world out, you could—by taking thought and common action—put it within a controlling context so that it could better serve the interests of the community. And, all through the last century, it was demonstrated that scenery, summer people, retired couples, taxes on tobacco, liquor, horse racing, and sweepstakes—while they help—are not enough to give a community an independent character of its own.

There is a precedent for dealing with that, too. From the very beginning, New Hampshire has been a society of small communities in which people set store by the local, the particular, and the personal. Throughout its history, this has been one of its principal attractions for those beyond its borders, and it is a special attraction today when the progress of the technological is toward the universal, the general, and the systematic. There is no reason why the indispensable and inevitable development of technology in the state (the appropriate parts of light industry) cannot be fitted suitably and attractively into the historic scheme, as were the old grist mill and textile mills.

All that is required is a community determined to make it happen. And there are precedents for that, as well—in some number. The first settlement around the Piscataqua, the long struggle to stand free of the Bay Colony, the self-contained order of the first thirty years of the nineteenth century, the mounting of the liberal and liberating spirit of the first decade of the twentieth century—all are testimony to the fact that members of a society acting in support of agreed-upon objectives can achieve their ends.

What, in fact, is being celebrated this year is an occasion that demonstrated, two hundred years ago, that the citizens of New Hampshire could so modify their remarkable diversity of interest and attitude that they could join together to create a new kind of life for themselves.

Suggestions for Further Reading

The first general history of New Hampshire was Jeremy Belknap's three-volume work, *The History of New Hampshire* (Boston: Belknap and Young, 1791–1792). It is still useful as a source of essential information and still impressive as a work of art. The last comprehensive history is J. Duane Squires, *The Granite State of the United States: A History of New Hampshire from 1623 to the Present*, 4 vols. (New York: American Historical Company, 1956). This work covers matters political, social, and economic, and contains useful bibliographies for each period.

For the political experience of New Hampshire up to 1789, Leonard W. Labaree, *Royal Government in America* (New Haven, Conn.: Yale University Press, 1930) supplies an excellent background in its careful description of colonial administration throughout the country before the Revolution. Otis G. Hammond, "The Mason Title and its Relations to New Hampshire and Massachusetts," an American Antiquarian Society Pamphlet (Worcester, Mass.: Davis Press, 1916) is the indispensable source of information for an understanding of the fundamental issue in the state's early settlement. Charles E. Clark, *The Eastern Frontier: the Settlement of Northern New England, 1610–1763* (New York: Alfred A. Knopf, 1970) contains much interesting material on the development of New Hampshire in the colonial period. Jere Daniell, *Experiment in Republicanism* (Cambridge, Mass.: Harvard University Press, 1970), based on extensive research in collections official and personal, is a balanced and resourceful account of the long train of events that led to self-government in the state. Richard F. Upton's *Revolutionary New Hampshire* (Hanover, N.H.: Dartmouth College Publications, 1936) is still the most useful source for the state's part in the struggle for independence.

For the politics of the nineteenth century, Donald B. Cole, *Jacksonian Democracy in New Hampshire, 1800–1851* (Cambridge, Mass.: Harvard University Press, 1970) and Richard H. Sewell, *John*

P. Hale and the Politics of Abolition (Cambridge, Mass.: Harvard University Press, 1971) are indispensable for an understanding of the antebellum period. Leon Burr Richardson, *William E. Chandler, Republican* (New York: Dodd, Mead and Company, 1940) deals primarily with the events of the last half-century; in the breadth and depth of its research, it is a model study of the political process and a remarkable public servant.

There are good books on various aspects of the economic life of the state. Robert G. Albion, *Forests and Sea Power* (Cambridge, Mass.: Harvard University Press, 1926) is a classic examination of the early timber trade, ably extended and supplemented by Joseph J. Malone, *Pine Trees and Politics, 1691–1715* (Seattle, Wash.: University of Washington Press, 1964). William A. Saltonstall, *Ports of Piscataqua* (Cambridge, Mass.: Harvard University Press, 1841) is the great source for information on early shipping and shipbuilding. William R. Brown, *Our Forest Heritage* (Concord, N.H.: New Hampshire Historical Society, 1958) deals with the timber industry and the life of the North Country. John B. Armstrong, *Factory Under the Elms, A History of Harrisville, New Hampshire* (Cambridge, Mass.: M.I.T. Press, 1969) is an extremely interesting and complete account of the life history of one of the family-owned mills that was typical in size and scale of so much of New Hampshire's textile industry in the nineteenth century. The dramatic exception in the state is described uncritically in G. W. Browne, *The Amoskeag Manufacturing Company of Manchester, New Hampshire* (Manchester, N.H.: The Amoskeag Manufacturing Company, 1915).

Among the series of statistical gazetteers that appeared periodically in the last century and in which can be found invaluable information bearing on what may be called the true condition of New Hampshire, a special word must be reserved for the work of Alonzo J. Fogg, *The Statistics and Gazetteer of New Hampshire* (Concord, N.H.: D. L. Gurnsey, Bookseller and Publisher, 1874). In addition to the usual numbers, computations, and descriptions, the book contains useful summaries of such subjects and activities as historical moments, railroads, crops, and the working press. It is also interspersed with beguiling opinions on the life and meaning of the state.

Index

Printed in the United States
102154LV00002B/40/P

9 780393 334104

Made in the USA
Monee, IL
09 April 2022

94425112R00142